ATOMIC ATTRACTION

ATOMIC ATTRACTION

The Psychology of Attraction

Christopher Canwell

RAMPAGE BOOKS

Develop Attraction
www.developattraction.com

ISBN 978-1-9998722-2-9

First Published by Rampage Books in 2017

Throughout this book I have included many case studies to help provide a deeper understanding of attraction and how it works in real-life situations. These case studies are all based to some degree on events and scenarios I have witnessed. All names, locations, and personal information have been changed for obvious reasons. Any similarity to other people or events is purely coincidental.

Set in Steelfish, DIN EngSchrift, Frutiger, Garamond, and Baskerville.

ABOUT THE AUTHOR

Christopher Canwell is a psychologist who specializes in attraction and relationships. He works with clients around the world and is the founder of Develop Attraction (a popular website that shows men how to harness the power of attraction to get what they want in life and relationships).

For more information visit:
www.developattraction.com

ACKNOWLEDGEMENTS

I owe a debt of gratitude to all the men I've interacted with both professionally and personally over the years. I've had the privilege to work with thousands of men, working together to help them solve their relationship problems. During this time, I've seen both the best and worst of humanity. I've seen men on the verge of suicide, I've seen families torn apart, and I've seen men restore relationships that in ordinary circumstances appeared broken beyond repair. I've witnessed thousands of relationship problems, failures, and successes from which predictable patterns of behavior began to emerge. I came to realize that as humans we are all different yet we are all the same. We are plagued by the same fears, the same hopes, the same goals, and the same ambitions. Without the honesty and insight provided by my clients, I would not have been able to write this book. With that said, the case studies in this book are all based on true events. Only names, locations, and personal information have been changed with permission from the people involved.

From a little spark may burst a flame.

— Dante

TABLE OF CONTENTS

INTRODUCTION

As you read through this book, keep in mind that the information found within these pages is not for the faint of heart. Getting results is all that matters; and to get results, you must be willing to face reality no matter how uncomfortable that reality might be. And while love is an emotional state of being that is accompanied by feelings of comfort, safety, and warmth, you're about to discover that attraction is anything but safe or comfortable—building attraction is a process that is both challenging and unsettling. If, however, you're one of the few men who can summon the strength of mind to accept the truths buried deep within this book, your potential to get what you want in life and relationships is well within reach. And although there are many tricks and superficial strategies you can use to build attraction such as walking a dog,[1] carrying a musical instrument,[2] and even bearing physical scars to make yourself appear more attractive[3]—this book is not about gimmicks— this book is about cutting through misconceptions to show you how to build real attraction—attraction that leads to more dates, more sex, and more love.

With that said, there is the illusion that women need love and commitment for attraction to exist. Men assume they must court a woman and be sweet and kind to her to capture her interest and stand out from the crowd. There is the all too pervasive belief that women are non-sexual beings who only engage in sexual intercourse to please men. An outdated belief? Perhaps. But these misconceptions are still, to this day, propagated by millions of nice guys around the world. These nice guys live under the illusion that if they are just that little bit more supportive and kind they will be handed the "keys to the kingdom" and receive unlimited sexual access to women.

Furthermore, political correctness has without doubt taken a toll on modern relationships. We live in a world where men are now more afraid than ever to act like men. Over the past several decades there has been an undeniable shift in Western society towards political correctness, feminism, and the suppression of masculine behavior. You only have to look as far as Hollywood and the mainstream media to see evidence of this cultural shift on an epic scale. The message is clear: do the right thing; man up; be a nice guy; buy her gifts; buy her flowers; be chivalrous; women are more precious and deserving than men; men are the root of all evil; if men didn't exist, there wouldn't be any wars; if you want to have sex with a woman, you're both a pervert and a creep. Sound familiar? This refrain, sung en masse, has not only corrupted and corroded society, causing a massive gender imbalance, it has also given birth to a sociological phenomenon known as *Nice Guy syndrome.*

If you live in the developed world and you're reading this there's a good chance you're a nice guy. You've been raised to honor and protect women. You don't want to hurt anyone's feelings. You want a real and authentic relationship where you can love, honor, and respect a woman with the expectation that she will do the same for you in return. There's only one problem—you've been sold a lie.

Men have moved so far away from their innate masculinity that they've lost sight of what it takes to attract women and capture a woman's interest. It's no surprise that approximately 50 percent of marriages end in divorce when the biological fabric of society has been ripped apart.[4] When you stop behaving in a way that's true to your masculine self, you repel women and drive them away. And instead of falling for Mr. Nice Guy, that beautiful woman ends up in the arms of Mr. Not So Nice (someone less caring, less kind, but a lot more attractive).

Sigmund Freud—the famous Austrian neurologist and founder of psychoanalysis—once said, "The great question that has never been answered, and which I have not yet been able to answer, despite my thirty years of research into the feminine soul, is what does a woman want?" Now, thanks to modern research we can finally answer this question. What do women want? What turns them on? Who do they find attractive? And what makes a woman fall in love? We now have the ability to answer these questions, and, more importantly, understand what turns a woman on and off. Ever wondered why that beautiful woman keeps dating assholes and unsavory characters? The answer, which you'll implicitly understand by the time you finish this book, is both surprising and counter-intuitive.

The world is full of misinformation and false prophets. It has become harder than ever to separate fact from fiction, especially where male/female relations are concerned. How do you deal with the inevitable tests, the unexpected withdrawals, the unresponsive behavior, and the inevitable loss of attraction that creeps into all relationships at some point in time? How do you meet a woman for the first time and generate attraction, and not only generate attraction but maintain it over the long-run? The purpose of this book is to answer all these questions by shining a light onto attraction so you can see it for what it is: your best friend or your worst enemy.

PART ONE

BECOME ATTRACTIVE

*Shallow men believe in luck; strong
men believe in cause and effect.*

— Ralph Waldo Emerson

Attractive people have easier lives. Attractive people make more money, get more promotions, get better jobs, have more friends, and have more sex.[5] An international study into attraction found that women are much more likely to go on a date, go to bed, or go to the apartment of a man who's rated "moderately high" or "highly" attractive. But as the study also discovered, these same women were unwilling to go on a date, go to bed, or go to the apartment of a man rated "less" attractive.[6]

At first, it's natural to assume a man must be physically handsome in much the same way a woman is physically beautiful to be considered attractive. Men often believe they don't have what it takes to be attractive; attraction isn't for them, it belongs to those ethereal creatures blessed with great physical beauty. You might think you're not tall enough, not talented enough, not interesting enough, and not good looking enough to be attractive. But as you're about to discover the nature of attraction is often deceptive. When a woman looks at a man she considers attractive, she isn't looking for a pretty face or beautiful features as so many advertising campaigns would have you believe. Instead, she's looking for indicators of strength and a "rugged visage" characterized, most prominently, by the presence of testosterone.

I would be doing you a huge disservice writing a book about attraction if I told you that looks don't matter. Human beings are superficial creatures, and when it comes to attraction, looks are undoubtedly important. Most men, however, assume that the features that make a woman attractive are the same features that make a man attractive—they are not. Men and women are attractive in different ways. Watch any advertising campaign or TV commercial and it's easy to be fooled into thinking that societies' view of male beauty is a man with a feminine face and soft features. Despite the fact the media often portrays feminine men as the ideal, it's safe to say that the vast majority of women don't find feminine men sexually attractive or appealing. In general, healthy, masculine features are the type of features women find most desirable. If you focus on cultivating beautiful features, yes, you might be considered handsome and aesthetically pleasing, but you'll do little to generate attraction.

One interesting study into facial attractiveness found that facially attractive men (meaning men with attractive masculine features) have better sperm quality than non-facially attractive men.[7] In most cases, when a man is considered facially attractive, this means he displays strong traces of testosterone characterized by the presence of facial hair, a thicker brow, and a broad chin. Testosterone tells a woman that a man has good genes and a healthy reproductive capacity.

Research carried out by the University of California, Davis discovered that women are looking for significantly fewer physical qualities compared to men when selecting a mate.[8] To further corroborate these findings, a study conducted by researchers at Aquinas College confirmed that the cognitive aspect of attraction is much more important to women than it is to men.[9] Women also tend to focus more on a man's behavior, personality, and attitude as a measure of attraction as opposed to his physical attributes. So, if a man's physical attributes are relatively unimportant in the realm of attraction, what is it about men that women find most attractive? And what is it that compels women to seek men out for love, sex, and reproduction?

Women, as the research shows, are looking for signs of strength and confidence. Every decision a woman makes concerning attraction comes back to one crucial point: can you, as a man, provide her with strong, healthy children? If the answer is *yes*, her child is more likely to grow up to be healthy, strong, and capable of reproduction, ensuring the longevity of the woman's genes well into the future. Every time a woman considers going on a date, having sex, and getting into a relationship, she is assessing, at a subconscious level, the strength of her date's DNA and his ability to create strong, healthy offspring.

Still, there are times when women choose to date

and marry men they don't find attractive. In this case, the woman opts to settle down with a beta male who's caring, nurturing, beta qualities make for an excellent provider. But are these women sexually attracted to their beta partners? The answer, of course, is a resounding *no*. The woman has simply chosen to settle down with a beta male as she seeks out stronger more confident men for sex and reproduction. This relationship dynamic provides women with the best of both worlds—a provider husband and the strongest possible DNA for her offspring. It is, at the same time, unfortunate that the beta male reaps few benefits in this arrangement with all the real, tangible benefits going to the woman and her alpha partner. Given a choice between an alpha male and a beta male, a woman will always choose to be with a strong, confident man for romance, marriage, and sex.

If your goal is to become more attractive, you must first understand the core elements of attraction. For instance, how can you emulate the behavior of an alpha male and attract more women into your life? At this point, it's important not to become fixated on attributes you can't change like your age, ethnicity, and height. (As an aside, it's interesting to note that men often assume that tall people are more attractive; however, a revealing study carried out by Ohio State University discovered that women don't prefer to date tall men, they just prefer to date men who are taller than themselves.[10] A man's height is, of course, relative to a woman's height.) Instead of focusing on those physical attributes you can't change, it's always better to think of female attraction for what it is in its purest form: women are attracted to *strength* and *masculinity*. Anything you can do to enhance your strength and masculinity will make you significantly more attractive to women.

CASE STUDY #1: MAKE AN IMPACT

Peter worked as an account executive for a large insurance company; and at age 35, he felt like he was doing pretty well for himself. He had a good income, a nice car, and a spacious condo overlooking the city.

One morning, Peter stopped by his favorite coffee shop on his way to work. As soon as he walked through the door, he saw her—a beautiful woman standing by the counter. Wow, Peter thought, she looks amazing. Peter stood by the entrance to the coffee shop, watching the woman's every move. Her delicate hands closed the lid on her coffee as she strolled right past him on her way out the door. Her perfume, sweet and flowery, lingered in the air long after she was gone. From that moment on, Peter was hooked. Peter decided there and then to make it a part of his daily routine to stop by the coffee shop every morning before work, where, at exactly 8:45 a.m., every Monday and Wednesday, the same woman would walk into the coffee shop and order a cappuccino with soy milk.

Every time Peter saw her, he felt intoxicated. She was so attractive, he knew he had to ask her out or he would go to his grave with a deep sense of regret for having let such a beautiful woman get away. Peter knew all he had to do was find a way to approach her and strike up a conversation. Unfortunately, this was easier said than done. Every time Peter tried to talk to this incredible woman, his body shut down. He had never felt this nervous around a woman before. *I guess it just goes to show how much I like her,* Peter mused.

The following week, after much deliberation, Peter finally summoned the courage to go up to the woman and say "hi" as she added a dash of cinnamon to her cappuccino. The woman turned and saw Peter standing beside her. Peter raised his coffee and smiled, "Hi, I'm Peter."

The woman gave Peter a faint, disinterested smile, then left the coffee shop without saying a word.

Peter stood by the counter, shocked and confused. He felt like his world was about to collapse. *She couldn't even bring herself to say hi,* he thought. *Am I that unattractive? Where did I go wrong? Maybe I didn't smile enough. Maybe she didn't hear me. No, that's not possible.* Peter was so upset and embarrassed he wished the ground would just open up and swallow him whole.

* * *

Three months later, the same woman was in the same coffee shop, adding a dash of cinnamon to her cappuccino when she heard an unfamiliar voice call out beside her—"Hey." The woman looked up and saw a man standing close by. The man was in his late-thirties, had a shaved head, and thick designer stubble. The woman was intrigued. The man didn't break eye contact as he looked directly into her eyes. *Wow,* she thought, *he's confident. Who is this guy?*

"Hi," the woman said.

The man reached out and touched her on the arm.

"You come here often?"

"Almost every morning," the woman gushed.

"What's your name?"

"Jane," the woman replied, flashing a smile.

"I'm Paul, nice to meet you."

* * *

Why, given their similar approach, did Jane dismiss Peter and accept Paul? The answer, as always, boils down to *attraction*. Paul displayed significantly more markers of attraction than Peter. For his part, Peter was still on the chubby side, even though he went to the gym three to four times a week. His clothes were a bad fit, and this signaled a serious lack of style and social awareness. Peter's prominent bald patch was also a turn-off, especially as it made him look like a corporate version of Friar Tuck. And finally, more than anything else, there was the obvious lack of confidence.

For the past two weeks, Peter had been lingering around the coffee shop, checking Jane out. Jane, who was no stranger to attention, had noticed Peter's presence and his frequent gaze in her direction. Once, when Peter was at the counter, ordering coffee, Jane had taken a moment to study him. He looked like a regular middle-aged guy. And although Peter was only in his mid-thirties, he looked 35 going on 50. From Jane's perspective, Peter was just another out of shape office worker strolling around in a bad suit.

In contrast, Paul was able to generate attraction with Jane in a matter of seconds. He displayed extreme confidence in his approach and never hesitated not even for a second. Surprisingly enough, from a physical perspective, Peter was naturally better looking than Paul. Paul had a receding hairline and in fact had less hair than Peter. Paul, however, shaved his head instead of letting it grow out. Paul also had thick stubble on his face, another key marker of testosterone. And then there was the suit. It was obvious that Paul knew enough about fashion to make a strong first impression. The fact that Paul was in excellent physical shape, and had a lean, muscular body didn't hurt either. Everything about Paul's appearance signaled strength, confidence, and masculinity.

ᛉ

A lot of men are intimidated by the concept of masculinity. This fear of the masculine is even more pronounced in today's politically correct, feminist society where a dominant left-wing media continues to promote nice guy values where men are expected to behave in a subservient, pleasing manner towards women. In reality, this weak, insecure behavior turns women off and results in a loss of attraction. So why are so many men afraid to embrace their masculinity and project strength? The truth often lies in the inherent belief that men don't feel like they have any real strength or masculinity to begin with. The modern man often feels weak and powerless; castrated by society and emasculated by women. Add to this the fact that society often portrays masculine traits as unattractive and antisocial and you can see why masculinity is in decline and feminism is on the rise. This aversion to masculinity often stems from the misconception that strength equals aggression.

Projecting strength is not about being aggressive or rude. It's not about being hostile and starting fights—nothing could be further from the truth. In fact, acting in this way is a sure sign of weakness and insecurity. A study into aggression by researchers at the University of South Florida found that men often overestimate another man's desire to want to resort to aggression when faced with conflict.[11] Men often have the misconception that acting in an aggressive and "macho" way is attractive to women and that aggression is often necessary to gain the respect of a man's peers (this is one reason why so much violence exists among gangs of young men).

Interestingly enough, research into aggression and attraction found that women view men as more desirable when they're less aggressive and able to solve problems in a more sophisticated way. After all, violence, unless under serious threat, is considered reckless since it comes with a high risk of punishment. And while it's true that women find dominant traits like *assertiveness* attractive, assertiveness should never be confused with aggression. Being cool, calm, and composed is much more attractive than being a reckless hot-head who flies off the handle at the slightest sign of provocation. True attraction is built on confidence, and a confident man only uses aggression as a last resort.

With that said, this section examines the traits you should focus on to make yourself appear more attractive and confident around women. You'll discover how to become more attractive by optimizing every aspect of your appearance from your body to your clothes. And once you know how to create a striking appearance, you'll be able to inspire the kind of attraction that melts hearts and arouses lust and devotion in equal measure.

BUILD A STRONG BODY

Everything is judged by its appearance;
what is unseen counts for nothing.

— Robert Greene

You've just been introduced to a man whose body is muscular and athletic. You look at this man and you're immediately impressed by his physique. His body looks primed as though ready to explode. When the man speaks, he has your immediate respect, not because he's dangerous, but because his presence sends a clear message: I'm worthy of respect. Simply by looking at this man you get a clear sense of his personality and character. You know for a fact that he's hard-working, focused, and persistent. After all, you don't build a strong body by being lazy, lying around on the couch, eating pizza all day. This man respects himself and his body. You also know for a fact that this man is mentally strong and doesn't shy away from hardship or pain. A strong body is, after all, a reflection of a strong mind. A man must be willing to sacrifice a degree of comfort for pain if he's to carve out a muscular physique. Most men prefer to take the easy route in life, not this man.

Now imagine you've just been introduced to a man who's overweight and out of shape. He cares little for his appearance and has a protruding belly and weak posture. He's also a heavy smoker and drinks a lot, which does nothing to endear him to women as a study published in the journal *Evolutionary Psychology* points out: women view men who smoke and drink to excess as significantly less attractive than nonsmokers and occasional drinkers.[12] The findings of this study indicate that smoking and drinking to excess are both forms of risky behavior that offer no long-term reward and few advantages. On the other hand, risky behaviors that bring rewards, such as starting a business or taking a loan for further study are viewed as much more attractive by women because they fall under the category of a "calculated risk."

As you look at the weak, overweight man in front of you, you instantly—and without even being aware of it—lose a measure of respect. The man's poor physique and excess body fat tell you all you need to know about his character. First, he's more likely to be lazy and gluttonous. Studies show that people who are overweight are more likely to be perceived as lazy and thus less attractive (this accounts for about two-thirds of the population in the West who are categorized as clinically overweight). Second, the fact that this man has allowed his body to deteriorate to such an extent indicates that the man has poor self-control.

The way you present yourself to the world reveals a lot about your character. Call it superficial and shallow, but human beings are programmed to pick up on physical cues, and to make mental shortcuts when evaluating other people. One of the best ways to display good genes and a healthy reproductive capacity is to develop a strong, muscular body. A study conducted by researchers at UCLA noted that women rate men with muscular physiques as more attractive and desirable.[13] The reason for this is simple. The man with a muscular physique projects strength, health, and good genes. Juxtapose this with the man who's weak, skinny, or overweight, and you can see why women find muscular men more attractive.

At this point it's important to note that a good muscular physique shouldn't be confused with a bad muscular physique. So, what exactly constitutes a bad muscular physique? If you've ever seen a man with over-sized arms, an enormous chest, a big bloated stomach, and skinny legs, you're looking at a man with a bad muscular physique. On the other hand, a good physique is well-balanced, symmetrical, and pleasing to the eye.

After dealing with hundreds of clients over the years and witnessing the benefits of working out first-hand, I'm of the belief that developing a strong body is one of the most important things a man can do to improve his life. Not only does working out improve your health, it also makes you look infinitely more attractive.

THE BENEFITS OF WORKING OUT

— You'll boost your immune system
— You'll increase your mental strength
— You'll increase your testosterone levels
— You'll become more sexually attractive
— You'll get more respect from men and women
— You'll increase your strength and bone density
— You'll project greater strength and masculinity
— You'll reduce your risk of depression and anxiety

A lot of men resist working out, often citing busy work schedules or hectic lifestyles as an excuse to avoid the gym. Keep in mind this way of thinking is indicative of the unattractive man. Research conducted by UCLA provides a healthy dose of motivation for men who are still reluctant to workout. The UCLA study examined how likely women are to pursue men who are "more muscular than average," or if muscles are even a factor when it comes to attraction. The results of the study found that women aren't just more attracted to men who are muscular; women are more likely to chase and pursue muscular men to have short-term affairs and romantic relationships.[14] Once you summon the mental fortitude to push through the initial pain barrier that comes with working out, you'll not only strengthen your body; you'll strengthen your mind as well, making you that much more attractive in the process.

CHOOSE THE RIGHT HAIRSTYLE

*Can't say it often enough—change
your hair, change your life.*

— Thomas Pynchon

When choosing the right hairstyle, it's important to
think about what makes you feel good as well as what
makes you look good. If you feel good wearing short
hair, this, in turn, will increase your confidence and
make you feel better about yourself. Nevertheless, the
goal of this book is to make you more attractive. To
achieve this end, your appearance must first and
foremost project masculinity. Thus, when it comes to
choosing the right kind of hairstyle, there are two
important considerations to keep in mind: first, short
hair projects masculinity; and second, long hair
projects a softer, more feminine look.

As a general rule, short to medium length hair will
help you project a more masculine image, especially
when complemented by light stubble or a beard. And
while long hair might make you look more handsome,
it will also make you look more feminine. If you're
unsure about what kind of hairstyle works best for
you, it's better to lean on the side of caution and keep
your hair short to project a more masculine image. If

you still want to grow your hair long, you can add a touch of masculinity to your appearance by letting your facial hair grow out. And just as you must be aware of the consequences of growing long hair, you must also be aware of the consequences of excessive grooming. Spend too much time grooming your hair and you'll leave the vast majority of women feeling uninspired and disinterested. If you over-style your hair you run the risk of coming across as cold, sterile, controlling, boring, predictable, stuffy, and overly focused on your appearance.

Surprisingly enough, women often express a fondness for men who let their hair grow a little wild and disheveled. Yes, be clean, yes, groom your hair, but don't focus on your hair to the point of perfection. The key to maintaining an attractive head of hair is to keep your hair short-to-medium length, healthy, and natural. And even more important than all these factors combined—you must choose a hairstyle that makes you feel good and instills you with confidence.

DEALING WITH GRAY HAIR

When you look in the mirror and see those first gray hairs sprouting from your head, the natural reaction is to panic and reach for the tweezers. Only a couple of months later, those pesky gray hairs keep coming back. Again, you reach for the tweezers... until eventually it dawns on you: you're fighting a losing battle. And while you might convince yourself that gray hair is something that only old men have to deal with, it's not uncommon for men in their early twenties and thirties to have gray hair, nor is it uncommon for men in their twenties and thirties to have a receding hairline. Men often believe that "going gray" spells the end of attraction. This fear, however, is all in the mind. In reality, the more mature and distinguished a man looks, the more opportunities he will have to seduce and attract women regardless of age.

A MATCH.com study found that 72 percent of women rated men with gray hair as "distinguished" and "hot."[15] Based on these results, you shouldn't fear the onset of gray hair; instead, you should embrace your "grayness" and the romantic opportunities that come with being a silver-haired fox. Nevertheless, if you have gray hair, it is important to keep your hair short. If you grow your hair long, gray hair tends to look thin and wiry compared to other types of hair.

Men who go gray in their twenties and thirties often have a hard time accepting this sudden change in their appearance. If you feel as though you're too young to go gray and you still have a full head of hair, one solution is to dye your hair to retain a more youthful appearance (just make sure you use a good quality hairy dye that matches your natural hair color). As a proviso, dyeing your hair should only be an option if you have less than 20 percent gray hair, any more than 20 percent and it will be difficult to conceal the gray for too long.

GOING BALD (MAN'S GREATEST FEAR)

Ninety-four percent of men listed going bald as one of their greatest fears.[16] Permanent hair loss is often seen as a sign that a man is getting old and is now "past his prime." At least that's what we're led to believe, but is it true? There's no doubt going bald does make a man look older, but it doesn't mean a man looks any less attractive. For men, youth doesn't equal attractiveness in the same way it does for women. That being said, once you start going bald, you have three options when it comes to dealing with hair loss:

Option one, stop hair loss by taking a Propecia/Finasteride pill every day for the rest of your life (this is the only medication that is scientifically proven to stop hair loss); option two, get a hair transplant to cover up those bald spots; and option three, embrace hair loss and shave your head.

Option one sounds tempting, doesn't it? After all, wouldn't it be great just to take a pill and stop hair loss dead in its tracks? And if it sounds too good to be true, it's because it is. Hair loss, also known as *male pattern baldness*, occurs in men when Dihydrotestosterone (DHT) reacts with the hair follicles in the scalp and shuts down normal hair production. Anti-hair loss medication like Propecia shuts down the production of Dihydrotestosterone (DHT), the sex hormone responsible for hair loss. Blocking DHT will prevent further hair loss and, in some cases, reverse hair loss. So why should you think twice about using Propecia as a viable hair loss solution? To shut down DHT production in your body, Propecia must first shut down your body's testosterone production. There's no way to avoid this. Every single man who takes Propecia to stop hair loss inhibits the production of testosterone in his body. Despite what the information on the box might tell you, it's impossible not to experience side-effects when your testosterone levels are depleted.

I've lost count of the number of men I've spoken to who've taken Propecia to combat hair loss only to report the following devastating side-effects: numbness in the testicles, shrunken testicles, erectile dysfunction, energy loss, loss of muscle mass, and loss of hardness in the body caused by reduced testosterone levels. I'm yet to hear of a single man who's taken Propecia over an extended period of time who hasn't experienced at least one of these side-effects. When you inhibit testosterone production, you're starving your body of the one key hormone the male body needs to function effectively—testosterone.

If you're considering option two, a hair transplant, this is a relatively safe albeit expensive procedure. You need to be aware, however, that in the case of hair transplants, there's a strong possibility that if you're still relatively young, your hairline might continue to recede well into the future. You should only consider a hair transplant if you're at least 30 years of age to limit the risk of further hair loss.

Now, let's consider option three: shaving your head. Over the years, I've spoken with dozens of men who blame a lack of sex and a lack of interest from women on hair loss. "If only I still had my hair," the balding man laments. "If I still had a full head of hair, women would still find me attractive." Of course, it's understandable to feel this way. After all, a lot of men experience ridicule and feelings of embarrassment the moment they start going bald. But going bald isn't ridiculous or unattractive; it's only ridiculous if you try to conceal it.

A man who walks around sporting a hairstyle that

resembles Friar Tuck will be the butt of countless jokes. The man who takes matters into his own hands and shaves what's left of his hair off is suddenly transformed into a hyper-masculine, attractive male. An interesting study conducted by researchers at the University of Pennsylvania found that men with shaved heads were rated more attractive, assertive, and masculine compared to men with a full head of hair.[17] The Pennsylvania study also discovered that men with bald heads consistently ranked higher on masculinity, strength, dominance, and leadership potential. All this to say, if you're going bald, it's possible to become more attractive simply by shaving your head. It's sexy, it's masculine, and women love it.

TO SHAVE OR NOT TO SHAVE?

Nothing makes her purr like a face full of fur.

— Unknown

Women are intrigued and captivated by men who sport facial hair. It might sound superficial and ridiculous to imagine that growing facial hair can make a man look more attractive. Numerous studies, however, show that facial hair is desirable and sexy. One such study, published in the *Journal of Evolution and Human Behavior* found that facial hair has a dramatic and positive effect on a man's appearance.[18] Men with heavy stubble or a beard were not only rated more masculine and assertive, they were also rated as healthier and more attractive.

A study comprised of 351 women found that heavy stubble is the most attractive facial hair a man can grow (this is around ten day's worth of growth). Researchers at the Evolution & Ecology Research Centre also made a note of the fact that facial hair is not only correlated with maturity and masculinity it's also correlated with high-levels of dominance and assertiveness.[19]

CASE STUDY #2: WHAT IS IT ABOUT FACIAL HAIR?

Gary was a regular clean-cut guy. He came from a middle-class, conservative family who espoused the virtues of good grooming and a neat appearance. His clothes were always pressed, his hair was always groomed, and his face was always smooth. Gary didn't like change, and that was part of the reason why he had kept the same look his entire life. When Gary looked in the mirror, he liked what he saw—a handsome, fresh-faced guy staring back at him. He was traditionally handsome and had a face that was both inoffensive and unthreatening.

Gary felt confident in his appearance, but there was one thing that bothered him. Even though he knew he was good-looking, he didn't get all that much attention from women. It was odd, Gary thought. Everything except my love life is awesome. And the few girlfriends I've had in the past have all left me feeling uninspired. Then, just as Gary was lamenting his romantic misfortune, something happened that would change his life forever. Gary contracted pneumonia. The illness put Gary out of action for almost a month. He couldn't work, he had a constant fever, and except for a week where he stayed in the hospital, Gary spent the rest of his time convalescing at home.

* * *

A month later, Gary was starting to feel better. On the weekend before he was due back at work, Gary decided to join some friends for dinner at a restaurant downtown. When Gary walked into the restaurant, his friends were surprised to see him. He looked different, and although he had lost weight, he also looked more rugged. One of Gary's friends said he looked "cool with stubble." Another friend said he looked like a "badass... in a good way." These unexpected compliments made Gary stop and think. Nevertheless, it wasn't until an attractive girl, sitting at a table on the far side of the restaurant, looked right over and flashed him a smile that Gary thought there might be something more to his new "badass" appearance. It was now only a matter of time before Gary ditched his old, nice guy image in favor of a more edgy, masculine vibe.

⋏

If you're a typical nice guy, your clean-cut image might be working against you. If you want to maximize your potential and become more attractive, never underestimate the power of facial hair when it comes to projecting masculinity. When you first read this, it's hard to imagine that growing stubble or a beard could have such a single, dramatic effect on appearance. What is it about facial hair and why is it so attractive to women?

At a basic level, facial hair signals masculinity, strength, and dominance as evidenced by the presence of testosterone. There is, however, a fear among nice guys that growing facial hair only makes a man look rough and disheveled. If you're tempted to think along these lines, keep this in mind—if you want to be perceived as attractive, you must project masculinity and strength at all times. Facial hair is an easy way to display masculinity and exhibit testosterone in much the same way that a peacock fans out its feathers to attract a mate.

IS PENIS SIZE IMPORTANT?

Women don't suffer from penis envy. Men do.

—Joseph Heller

There isn't a man alive who hasn't, at some point, worried that his penis wasn't big enough or virile enough to satisfy a woman. Penis size is a major source of concern for men. Men worry that their penis isn't the right size, they worry that their penis isn't the right shape, and they worry that their penis doesn't have what it takes to bring a woman to orgasm. The truth is, the majority of penises when measured fall within just a couple of centimeters of each other.

The most extensive study on penis size, published in the *British Journal of Urology*, measured 15,521 penises around the world (including Africa, the Middle East, Europe, and North America). The results of the study found that the average penis was 5.2 inches in length with a circumference of 4.6 inches.[20] Men in the 25th or 75th percentile—meaning men who were either 25 percent smaller or larger than average—were only one centimeter bigger or smaller than the average 5.2 inches. Extremely small or large penises were rare. Only 5 percent of participants had a penis larger than 6.3 inches, and less than 5 percent of participants had a penis smaller than 3.9 inches.

Further research found that women when viewing

digitally altered pictures of the same man with a different sized penis, didn't rate the man with the largest penis or smallest penis as the most attractive; the women rated the man with the intermediate or "average" sized penis as the most attractive.[21] The most extensive penis size study in history reveals that most male penises are approximately the same size (give or take a couple of centimeters).

The penis is the one part of the male anatomy that stands alone as penis size is neither correlated with body mass index, foot size, hand size and is only slightly correlated with height. There are, of course, outliers, and men with large and small penises do exist, but these men are the exception, not the rule. And while women have a preference for proportionally sized penises (relative to a man's body), penis size isn't an issue that should cripple your ability to meet and date attractive women, nor should it prevent you from getting intimate with a woman and providing her with a sexually satisfying experience.

Men who constantly worry about the size of their penis and their ability to satisfy a woman are more likely to suffer erectile dysfunction and experience lower levels of confidence as a result. If a woman thinks you're insecure about the size of your penis, even if it's not an issue or a problem for her, she might one day decide to use your "penis anxiety" against you. You mustn't let concerns about your penis or its size be a source of weakness. According to science, there's a 95 percent chance you've got nothing to worry about.

AGE AND ATTRACTION

*Men are like wine—some turn to vinegar,
but the best improve with age.*

— Pope Adam XXIII

There's a long-held assumption that as a man gets older, his looks, virility, and physical appearance all take a turn for the worse. The belief that age erodes attraction is one of the most prevalent myths out there. Research, however, indicates that as a man gets older he often becomes more attractive.[22] And where a woman is considered to be in her physical prime in her twenties, a man is considered most attractive between the ages of 25 and 40. Unlike women who are judged mostly on their physical appearance, a man's attractiveness is based on a combination of skill, appearance, confidence, status, and experience.

Further research into age and attraction shows that women, on average, find older men more attractive than younger men.[23] These findings hold true even if a woman is financially independent and self-sufficient, suggesting that even when a woman has the freedom to choose her romantic partner without financial considerations, she will still choose to be with an older man who is more likely to be fun and possess greater experience and wisdom.[24] And while most men don't hit their prime until they're in their thirties or forties, a lot of men are already out of shape and physically unattractive by this age. This is usually a result of too much alcohol, smoking, and junk food consumption. As a general rule, the more overweight and out of shape a man is the more difficult it will be for him to attract and date beautiful women (unless the man has exceedingly high levels of status and wealth to compensate for his physical shortcomings).

In contrast, men who workout on a regular basis and eat healthy food can stay in excellent shape well into their forties, fifties, and sixties. If you look after yourself and remain young at heart, don't be surprised if you're still dating young and attractive women well into middle-age. It's certainly not uncommon for high-status men in their fifties and sixties to date young, beautiful women in their early twenties. A man is only limited by his beliefs and his imagination. Getting older is not something to be feared but something to be embraced.

DATING YOUNGER WOMEN

Women who date older men are often more feminine than women who date men of a similar age. In fact, the greater the age difference the more feminine a woman is likely to be. Feminine women often seek out older men as partners because this relationship dynamic feels more natural to their feminine soul. If you want to keep a younger woman attracted to you, you must exude masculine traits like leadership, confidence, and decisiveness. Where younger men are known for their indecisiveness, uncertainty, and false confidence, an older man must stand out with his years of experience, strength, and confidence.

If a woman senses uncertainty and weakness, then she'll pull away from you and look for a man who's stronger and more confident. The same applies if you try to seek reassurance from a woman about whether or not she loves you and is attracted to you. It's not uncommon for confident, attractive men to become weak and insecure the moment they start dating a young woman. These same men worry that they look too old, they worry that their girlfriend will leave them for a younger (more handsome) man, and they worry that their relationship is too good to be true and it's only a matter of time before their partner realizes she's dating an "old man."

The moment you start doubting yourself is the moment you open up Pandora's Box and bring unnecessary problems into your relationship. Remember, thoughts are energy and they hold real-world consequences. Age isn't a problem unless you make it a problem. Men who successfully date younger women never focus on age. Instead, they keep the relationship light, fun, and relaxed, and they never try to lock a woman into commitment before she's ready. If you want to date younger women, you mustn't let a small thing like age difference get in the way.

A SEDUCTIVE VOICE

*The human voice is the most beautiful instrument
of all, but it's the most difficult to play.*

— Josh Strauss

Researchers at University College London (UCL)
found that deep voices command more respect and
are more memorable than high pitched voices. Deep
voices were also found to resonate more with women.
The UCL researchers concluded that women find
deep voices attractive because deep voices appear to
signal that a man possesses high levels of
testosterone.[25] The study also noted that deep voices,
when tempered with a "breathy" quality, were rated
as the most attractive because these voices signal lower
levels of hostility and aggression.

An excellent way to develop a more commanding
and authoritative voice is to take slow, deep breaths
and speak from your diaphragm as opposed to
speaking from your throat. Most men tend to speak
from the throat or directly from the mouth without
utilizing the full power of their diaphragm. When
you're feeling tense or nervous, your muscles will
automatically tighten, and your breathing will become
fast and shallow. This results in a high-pitched
speaking voice. If you find yourself in a stressful or
uncomfortable situation where you need to
communicate, it's important to make a conscious

effort to slow your breathing and relax your muscles, especially around the shoulders. Speaking directly from the diaphragm helps to ensure your voice comes out in its full, natural tone—a tone that women find most seductive.

SMELLS THAT SEDUCE

Smell is the sense of memory and desire.

— Jean-Jacques Rousseau

Since Roman times, men have adorned themselves with scents and fragrances to attract the attention of beautiful women. Indeed, what every man wants to know is whether or not there's a magic scent he can use to attract women with ease. In the world of fragrances, a chemical compound called *hedione*—first used by Christian Dior in their iconic fragrance Eau Sauvage—was found to stimulate an area of the brain in women responsible for the release of sex hormones.[26] Hedione is now found in many well-known fragrances like CK One, Paco Rabanne's Invictus, Acqua di Gio, and Voyage d'Hermes.

There is, however, another type of smell that's even more powerful and effective than hedione. I am, of course, talking about testosterone, or more precisely, androstadienone. Androstadienone is a pheromone derived from testosterone (naturally found in men with high levels of testosterone). So how exactly does androstadienone work and what does it do? A fascinating study published in *Nature Neuroscience* found that female mice, when exposed to the smell of dominant alpha mice, underwent a form of neurological change after only two days.[27] After being exposed to alpha mice, the female mice would refuse to have anything more to do with the other beta/omega mice. The brains of the female mice had essentially been rewired to attach and mate with alpha mice only. There is evidence to suggest that women react much the same way after being exposed to the scent of alpha males.

Androstadienone also has another powerful effect on the female brain. Exposure to androstadienone has been found to trigger cortisol in women. This cortisol release can induce euphoria, shed inhibition, and reduce uncertainty and psychological concerns regarding a sexual partner. Another study published in the journal *Hormones and Behavior* found that women who were exposed to androstadienone for approximately fifteen minutes would become "subtly" more attentive, aroused, and happy.[28] With this research in mind, let's take a moment to look at some ways to increase the amount of natural testosterone in your body so you, too, can harness the benefits of androstadienone.

— Get good sleep and lots of rest
— Consume more zinc and vitamin D
— Eat a healthy diet with sufficient protein
— Reduce alcohol consumption, as alcohol is extremely estrogenic and toxic
— Reduce excess body fat through diet and exercise
— Use intermittent fasting to reduce insulin spikes and release more HGH (Human Growth Hormone)
— Eat more healthy fats (like peanut butter, olive oil, almonds, avocados, red meat, eggs, and dark chocolate)
— Workout in the gym, focusing more on compound

movements (like the squat, deadlift, bench press + high-intensity interval training)

It's also advisable to include garlic in your diet as a team of researchers in the Czech Republic discovered that men who regularly consume one to two cloves of garlic a day smell more attractive to women.[29] Garlic contains many antioxidants that improve the bodies metabolic functioning. These antioxidants reduce body odor, and garlic's powerful antibacterial properties help kill off strong smelling microorganisms while boosting the body's immune system at the same time.

Another study published in the *International Journal of Cosmetic Science* found that men who use a scented fragrance in day-to-day life feel more attractive and confident compared to men who don't wear any fragrance at all.[30] In the study, the researchers recorded silent video of the male participants either "wearing" or "not wearing" a fragrance. The researchers then showed the video footage to different groups of women. The women all rated the men who wore a fragrance as more attractive than the men who didn't wear any fragrance at all (even though the women had no way of knowing from watching the video whether the men were wearing a fragrance or not). The researchers claimed that the men who wore a fragrance must have acted more confident and thus appeared more attractive on video.

After reviewing this information, you can see how it's possible to increase the amount of natural testosterone in your body, and, in return, produce greater quantities of androstadienone (a pheromone that's been found to attract women and lower their defenses). Also, if you apply a cologne that contains hedione, a powerful combination takes place—you'll not only smell more attractive, you're also more likely to behave in a way that's more attractive as well.

CLOTHES THAT CAPTIVATE

Clothes make the man.

— Mark Twain

One of the surest ways to gain influence and become more attractive is to wear the right type of clothes. People believe what they see, and they're quick to cast judgment and make assumptions based on clothing and appearance alone. Like it or not, clothes matter. The airline pilot who wears a pilot's uniform is seen as skilled, professional, intelligent, and successful. A con man who wears the same pilot's uniform is viewed the same way—skilled, professional, intelligent, and successful.

If you know how to dress in style, you have a clear and distinct advantage in the realm of seduction. To better demonstrate this point, an interesting study published in David J. Buller's book *Adapting Minds*[31] examined the type of relationship a woman was willing to have with a man depending upon the type of clothes he was wearing (these clothes were either "low," "medium," or "high-status"). The type of relationship the woman was willing to enter into was separated into six different categories: (1) coffee and conversation; (2) a date; (3) sex only; (4) serious involvement, marriage potential; (5) sexual and serious, marriage potential; and (6) marriage. The goal of this study was to examine the effect clothes had on women's responses. The results of the study found that women were more attracted to the (same) man when his clothes were "high-status." So far, no surprise there; however, the study also discovered that women were much more likely to consider the man in all six categories if his clothes were "high-status" as opposed to "low" or "normal" status. In other words, if you're looking for a one night stand: wear high-status clothes; if you're looking for a long-term relationship: wear high-status clothes.

Further research has found that women find men who are well-dressed to be sexier, more intelligent, successful, more popular, and better relationship material. These findings provide striking evidence that clothes really do make a difference. In fact, wearing "high-status" clothes is one of the easiest ways for a man to become instantly more attractive to women. Still, this information is useless if you don't know how to choose the right types of clothes to enhance your appearance.

CHOOSING THE RIGHT CLOTHES FOR YOU

When choosing clothes that will make you look more attractive, your most important consideration is to decide what type of image you want to project? If you're the nerdy, intellectual type it would be a mistake to try and pull off the edgy, biker look. At the same time, if you're covered in tattoos, trying to dress like Poindexter would do nothing to enhance your appearance. At this point, you might be tempted to ask whether or not there's one type of look that works for every man? As a rule, it's always better to dress well (and it's always better to overdress than to underdress).

An insightful study conducted by Kelton Research found that women view men who dress up as sexier, smarter, and more successful.[32] What was even more interesting about this study was that 85 percent of women thought a well-dressed man was sexier than a man with a lot of money. Dressing well shows that you're socialized and socially intelligent—two characteristics that are attractive to women. The Kelton Research study also discovered that three out of every four men were underdressed most of the time. Of course, it's more comfortable to stroll around in a comfortable shirt and baggy shorts, but how do you expect to stand out when every other man is dressed the same way?

The purpose of this book is not to turn hordes of men into *fashionistas*, the purpose of this book is to help you increase your sexual market value, and, at the same time, help you improve your overall appearance so you become more attractive. Choosing the right clothes is one way to achieve this goal. This means you must first eliminate all clothes from your wardrobe that make you look unattractive. If your wardrobe is filled with clothes that are either too tight or too loose, you might as well throw them in the trash or donate them to charity because these clothes are killing your image.

Wearing suits, fitted shirts, and dress shirts will make you look more professional and successful. And where once women barely noticed you, your new appearance puts you firmly on the female radar. The wonderful thing about suits, fitted shirts, and dress shirts is that they work for all men, regardless of height, size, age, appearance, and ethnicity. Whether you're a biker covered in tattoos or a full-blown nerd, a good suit or fitted shirt will, without doubt, improve your appearance. And while you might be reluctant to sacrifice casual attire for something dressier, you must consider the rewards for being well dressed, not just in your relationships but in your personal and professional life as well.

When putting your wardrobe together, your number one priority is to make sure your clothes fit and look good. There are countless fashion magazines and websites out there from which to draw inspiration. I encourage you to browse these magazines and websites to get an idea of the type of clothes that look good on men. And when it comes to trying clothes on, don't be tempted to buy something just because you "think" it will look good or because it's on sale. Your clothes must fit, and they must fit you well. Just because an item of clothing looks good on the rack doesn't mean it will fit you or even look good on you.

A good way to begin your journey into fashion is to start by focusing on the fundamental elements of style. In this case, suits, dress shirts, and fitted shirts look great on just about every man who's in shape. Once you feel comfortable with these clothes and have developed an eye for what works and what doesn't, you can branch out into other areas of fashion to flesh out your wardrobe and give it more depth. You must never underestimate the power of dressing well for a well-dressed man is an attractive man.

THE BENEFITS OF DRESSING WELL

— Women will notice you
— You'll feel more confident
— You'll look more successful
— You'll get more immediate respect
— You'll act in a more attractive way
— You'll make a great first impression
— You'll be perceived as more attractive
— Women will be more interested in you

As you can see, the benefits are tangible and real, and your renewed sense of style will change the way you're perceived by women and the world around you. This book encourages you to step outside your comfort zone; if you can do this, the rewards and benefits are yours for the taking. Nonetheless, before you consider making any further changes to your wardrobe, you must also be aware of some crucial fashion mistakes that are known to kill attraction.

— Bad color coordination
— Wearing clothes that don't fit
— Wearing clothes that are too tight
— Wearing oversized suits and shirts
— Fastening all the buttons on your shirt
— Wearing sportswear on a regular basis
— Wearing clothes with large logos and slogans

If you can avoid these fashion mistakes, you'll not only sharpen your image, you'll strike a powerful first impression as well. At this point, it's important not to confuse "peacocking" with being fashionable and stylish. The man who peacocks (overdressing or dressing flamboyantly to attract attention) puts himself at severe risk of not only attracting the wrong kind of attention, he also risks looking ridiculous at the same time. Peacocking not only invites ridicule, it makes a man look desperate. Understated charm and elegance never goes out of fashion.

THE MOST ATTRACTIVE COLORS

Take a moment to consider the impact of color on attraction. Knowing what colors women find attractive goes a long way when it comes to creating a strong first impression and choosing the right clothes to enhance your appearance. An enlightening study published in the *Journal of Experimental Psychology* found that women are more attracted to the color red.[33] Red has been a symbol of power since Roman times. The most powerful men in Rome were known as *Coccinati*—meaning "the ones who wear red." The inclusion of red shirts, ties, scarves, and pocket squares in your wardrobe are sure to enhance your appearance and help you stand out from the crowd as women from the US, England, Germany, and China all rated men more attractive when they wore the color red.

Another study published in *Evolutionary Psychology* examined the effect of color on attraction in more detail.[34] Once again, red was found to be the most attractive color alongside black. The reason why these colors are so popular, however, remains something of a mystery. Although the researchers of the study speculated that red and black are colors that look good on most people and that these colors possibly have some evolutionary significance, purveying greater masculinity and strength on the wearer. The same study also discovered that women found the following colors the most attractive (in order of preference): red, black, blue, green, yellow, and white.

When choosing the right type of clothes to enhance your appearance, selecting the right colors is an important consideration that mustn't be overlooked. The moment you take control of your appearance, you immediately stand out, for a well-dressed man is not only physically appealing but psychologically appealing as well.

MONEY AND STATUS

Money without brains is always dangerous.

— Napoleon Hill

Men often believe that they don't have any real-world value unless they have money or status. Look around and it's easy to see why a man might feel this way, especially in a world that is often obsessed with fame and fortune. The world can be a shallow place, and it's no secret that the majority of cultures and countries hold people with wealth and status in high esteem. Men who have money and status are often seen as a "catch" compared to men who are less prosperous. As we dig deeper into the phenomenon of wealth and status, however, it soon becomes clear that it's the "prestige" element of status, not the "money" element that women find most attractive.

A study published by researchers at the University of North Carolina observed that wealthy men and attractive women are more likely to enter into relationships with each other.[35] But these relationships are often plagued by doubt and insecurity. I have personally consulted with many wealthy men who live in a state of constant fear and anxiety as they struggle to keep their girlfriends and wives happy. Despite spending thousands of dollars, these men often discover that money by itself is not enough to maintain attraction. Money, it turns out, is no cure-all or panacea for the absence of attraction.

The occasional gold digger aside, money doesn't make a man more attractive and desirable. Instead, it's the qualities and character traits that make a man wealthy that women find attractive, not the money itself. These positive qualities and character traits are especially prevalent in self-made men. And unless a man inherits his wealth, a wealthy man is more likely to be intelligent, determined, focused, strong, and confident for without these qualities it's unlikely he would have become wealthy in the first place. The man's wealth, in this case, is a form of social proof. At this point, it's important to note that women aren't just attracted to high-status men, women are also attracted to men who exhibit unrealized potential and ambition. In other words, an ambitious poor man is infinitely more attractive than a lazy rich man. In a world of talkers, the man who takes action stands out from the crowd.

YOUR SEXUAL MARKET VALUE

*Sex appeal is fifty percent what you've got and
fifty percent what people think you've got.*

— Sophia Loren

An unattractive, nervous man walks up to a woman
and says: "Hi, how are you?" almost stumbling over
his words. The woman looks at the man and without
uttering a single word in response walks off, leaving
the man feeling dejected and worthless.

The next day, an attractive, confident man walks
up to the same woman and says the exact same words:
"Hi, how are you?"

The woman looks at the man and smiles: "I'm
good, how about you?" This is the power of sexual
market value. The unattractive man has low sexual
market value, while the attractive, confident man has
high sexual market value. Why are successful actors
and professional athletes so attractive to women?
Because their celebrity status automatically confers
high-value. They have near unlimited options with
women. They are wealthy, successful, and (sometimes,
but not always) talented.

You don't have to be a celebrity, however, to
attract beautiful women into your life, but you do
have to increase your sexual market value. When a
woman rejects a man because he's overweight, is she
rejecting him because she's a shallow, superficial

person or is there another more profound explanation? The truth is, the overweight man gets rejected because his excess body fat sends the message that he doesn't respect himself. Any man who allows himself to become overweight and unattractive obviously doesn't care about his appearance. Second, excess body fat indicates a lack of drive and poor self-control. An overweight body is an indicator of general laziness and a lack of ambition. Most attractive women won't consider dating an overweight man unless the man is highly skilled, talented, or wealthy.

While it might be tempting, at this point, to label women superficial and shallow for behaving this way, it must be noted that just because a behavior appears superficial doesn't mean that behavior serves no purpose. As with all human behavior, there's often more going on beneath the surface than first meets the eye. For example, developing your body is the superficial development of muscle. Dig deeper, however, and you'll soon discover that improving your physique sends a much more powerful message. The man with a good physique is telling the world he's strong, healthy, has good genes, self-respect, ambition, focus, and persistence. Growing your facial hair, again, might at first appear superficial, but in reality, facial hair communicates masculinity, health, and the presence of testosterone. A smell might offer little more than a pleasant aroma, but as you now know, scents and fragrances communicate much more than the superficial. The right scent signals cleanliness, good grooming, social intelligence, health, testosterone, sexual compatibility, and masculinity. And as for clothes, isn't all that focus on fashion superficial and feminine? We now know that the benefits of being well-dressed extend far beyond the superficial. Stylish clothes project power, influence, social intelligence, style, glamor, and socialization.

As you raise your sexual market value, you increase the likelihood that women will find you attractive. At a rudimentary level, low sexual market value leads to fewer dating options, and high sexual market value leads to increased dating options. Women of childbearing age are looking for men they can reproduce with and thus give birth to strong, healthy offspring.

From a woman's perspective, the supply of high-value men is severely limited. As men, we are all the same, yet we are all different. We all experience the same emotions and have the same desires. We all want sex, love, affection, security, happiness, excitement, and adventure. We all experience loss, sorrow, despair, defeat, and uncertainty. These are the similarities that bind us together, regardless of race, age, and ethnicity. At the same time, we are all different. We all have different levels of education, wealth, physical ability, risk tolerance, drive, ambition, confidence, and opportunity. These are just some of the differences that separate the high-value man from the low-value man.

The low-value (beta) male is all too common. He's the majority, not the exception. In a world where it's easier to follow others than to take control of your life, the low-value man prevails. In a world where it's easier to be sedentary than to workout, the low-value man is the norm. In a world where it's easier to be lazy than to be ambitious, the low-value man thrives.

A study into perceived attractiveness published in the journal *Evolution and Human Behavior* found that women rated men who were lazy and unambitious as less attractive.[36] When the supply of high-value men is limited, the demand for high-value men increases as a result. A high-value man is cherished, adored, respected, and desired. Unfortunately, the reality is that not every man can be high-value. This is one of the brutal truths of attraction.

Most men stumble through life taking the path of least resistance. They are happy to live in this state, as this state requires little effort or risk. Most men seek shortcuts and instant gratification. One distinct difference that separates high-value men from low-value men is the high-value man's propensity to take risks and invest more effort into life. This extra effort on the part of the high-value man is what separates him from lesser men. A man with high sexual market value continually strives to improve himself both physically and mentally. It's a mistake to think women are only attracted to men who are successful. It's precisely this kind of thinking that leads to the crippling "she's out of my league" mentality.

Women aren't just attracted to men who are successful and ambitious—women are attracted to men who show "unrealized potential." A man who displays ambition, persistence, drive, energy, creativity, and a sense of purpose is more likely to be successful in the future. In other words, you don't have to be successful at this present moment in time to get the girl; you just have to create the perception that you have what it takes to be successful in the future. Whether or not you become successful is beside the point.

Most men, however, can only dream—they dream of getting the perfect girl, the perfect house, the perfect job, all the while falling short of realizing their full potential. The fundamental laws of physics dictate that you must take action to influence the world around you. What you think is of little consequence unless you have the ability to turn your thoughts into actions. The world of thoughts and emotions is a woman's world, a world that's ever-changing and uncertain. The world of men is a world of action. Men who take action have something that women crave—stability, strength, and purpose.

The purpose of this book is to show you how to become irresistible to women and maintain attraction in both short and long-term relationships. At this point, we've already discussed how to increase your sexual market value at a superficial level by projecting strength and masculinity. This is still not enough—you must embody strength. You must live and breathe it. You must learn to embrace your inner bad guy if you're to transform yourself into the kind of man that women find irresistible.

GOOD GUYS VS. BAD GUYS

Why do bad guys have all the fun? If there's one thing that separates the attractive bad guy from the unattractive good guy, it's that attractive men are never weak around women. If you're weak around women, even if you're rich, successful, and handsome, women will lose attraction for you. If a woman smells weakness, she'll pull away. If a woman feels she can control and manipulate you, she'll abuse you and try to control you. If a woman feels as though you'll do anything to please her, she'll lose respect for you.

It's at this point that you must ask yourself two important questions: first, how can a man be perceived as strong by women (or become what is commonly known as alpha)? And second, is a man born alpha or does he become alpha over time? Is alpha, in other words, a result of nature or nurture? In my own experience, alpha, as I've come to see it, is a trait that's mostly developed over time through conscious effort and awareness. Alpha versus beta is strength versus weakness. The beta male is weak; the alpha male is strong. The alpha male consistently chooses strength over weakness; the beta male chooses weakness over strength. The alpha male takes the strongest course of action; the beta male takes the weakest course of action. But how do you know what actions are strong and what actions are weak? Let's take a look at some different scenarios that better demonstrate this point in more detail:

Scenario #1: Your girlfriend tells you she wants to break up with you. What is the strongest course of action you can take and what is the weakest course of action?

The weakest course of action is to beg and plead with your girlfriend to stay in the relationship. The strongest course of action is to walk away with your head held high—this is the path of the alpha male.

Scenario #2: A woman doesn't respond to your text messages.

The weakest course of action is to send more messages. The strongest course of action is to walk away and ignore her until she gets back in touch with you.

Scenario #3: Your girlfriend tells you she just wants to be friends.

The beta male accepts the offer of friendship, hoping things will change in the future. The alpha male, again, walks away and ignores his girlfriend until she changes her mind.

Whenever you're in any doubt about how you should interact with women, ask yourself one important question: what's the strongest course of action I can take? If you're being honest with yourself, you already know the answer. Strong actions and behaviors are actions and behaviors that make you feel good about yourself. If you choose the strongest course of action in all areas of life, it won't be long before you project an alpha mindset without even thinking about it. At first, adopting an alpha mindset is a conscious decision, but over time this thought process becomes a natural part of who you are. An alpha mindset endures not just because it's guaranteed to get you more women and more sex, an alpha mindset endures because it's the right path to follow. It's the path to self-respect, freedom, and dignity. And just as weakness is the ultimate attraction killer, strength is the ultimate aphrodisiac.

The "nice guy" beta male who tries to please women by pretending to be kind and chivalrous does nothing to instill attraction. All he does is conceal his true thoughts and feelings. In reality, the nice guy is not nice. He's lying to himself about what he wants, and he's lying to the world around him. The nice guy pretends he just wants to be friends with women, even though being friends is the last thing on his mind. The nice guy thinks that by being nice, women will be compelled to like him in return. The nice guy rushes to a woman's defense with the hope that she'll reward him for his chivalry. The nice guy says he's not interested in sex when it's all he ever thinks about. This is in contrast to the "bad guy" alpha male who does the exact opposite. The alpha male doesn't care if people like him or not. The alpha male has no interest in defending women or saving them. The alpha male makes it clear that he's interested in sex and that he would love nothing more than to be intimate with a woman. As you can see, the bad guy is not really a bad guy, he simply speaks a truth that few men dare speak.

An alpha male embraces all that is masculine. He doesn't care what society thinks or what his family, friends, and other people think. The alpha male walks his own path and marches to the beat of his own drum. If he wants something, he goes after it. If he wants to become intimate with a woman, he lets her know without worrying about rejection. Part of the reason why alpha males can feel so confident and self-assured is that they don't rely on other people for validation. An alpha male never seeks validation from women; therefore, women are unable to rattle him or affect his confidence in any way. The alpha male also lives in a state of abundance. If a woman rejects him, it's no big deal. There are plenty more fish in the sea.

Most men are scared. They live their lives in a constant state of fear and anxiety. What happens if I get rejected? What happens if my wife leaves me? What happens if I lose my job? These are just a handful of fears men struggle with on a daily basis. But why are men so afraid? Men are afraid because they believe they have limited options in life, which, in turn, makes them feel powerless and helpless. The man who's afraid to lose his job believes he has limited economic opportunities, even in a world of financial abundance. The man who's scared his wife or girlfriend will leave him has the misguided belief that he'll never find a woman better than his current partner.

Women can smell weakness like a shark smells blood. When you see yourself as weak, helpless, and powerless, women can't help but see you the same way. In my discussions with men who've successfully made the transition from beta to alpha, I've noticed that these men all share one thing in common: they embrace masculinity. Some men are born alpha; for the majority of men, however, becoming alpha requires work (work that's both highly rewarding and satisfying).

Making the transition from beta to alpha always begins with the body. Strengthen your body and you strengthen your mind. The moment you start to feel powerful in your body is the moment you start to think with strength and certainty. When you feel vulnerable, you become vulnerable. When you see yourself as attractive, you become attractive. Your thoughts are manifested into reality, and you choose the path that ultimately determines your reality. In a world of beta males, the alpha male is king. You must never be afraid to go after what you want, even if it means ruffling a few feathers along the way.

Scientific research has discovered that men who are arrogant, selfish, cunning, manipulative, and over-confident enjoy a greater number of sexual partners and are viewed as infinitely more attractive by women. Women are also more attracted to men who display more dominant characteristics. One of the main problems with dominance is that it's often misconstrued as aggression. So, what is the best way to define dominance? A study conducted by the University of New Mexico attempted to break dominance down into three distinct components: social, financial, and physical.[37] In the New Mexico study, the researchers discovered that women rated physically dominant men high in both attractiveness and social dominance. The effect of financial dominance on attraction, however, was found to be inconsistent to the extent that financial dominance in and of itself was not a reliable indicator of attraction.[38] The New Mexico study also discovered that attractiveness was strongly correlated with the number of one-night stands a man was likely to have. Another study published in the *Journal of Personality and Social Psychology* discovered that dominant men were often perceived as sexually attractive, yet dominance had no effect on the man's overall level of likability.[39]

Exploring this topic further, a study carried out by UCLA researchers came to the conclusion that given a choice between a "dominant" man or a "prestigious" man, women have a definite preference for prestigious men.[40] Prestigious men are still dominant, but they're dominant in a different way. A prestigious man is neither aggressive nor violent; he's too smart and efficient to indulge in such high-risk/low reward behavior. Instead, the prestigious man constantly strives to raise his value in the world. He has clear and specific goals. Whether or not he's already achieved his goals is immaterial. Having a clear path and having direction in life is crucial when it comes to raising prestige. And as the UCLA research shows, being prestigious is much more attractive than being dominant.

Further research published by researchers at the University of California, Irvine suggests that women who are more sensitive and submissive are viewed as more attractive by men.[41] In fact, any time a person displays behaviors that are consistent with their gender norms (for example, men displaying leadership qualities, and women acting submissive and demure) that person is more likely to be seen as desirable by the opposite sex. Put simply, men are attracted to women who project feminine qualities, and women are attracted to men who project masculine qualities.

Another unexpected and enlightening aspect of the research into attraction is that selfishness often makes men appear more attractive. Being strategically selfish and assertive lets women know that you're more likely to acquire resources and thus more likely to become successful. Your success is, after all, not only your success but your partner and your offspring's success as well.

Consider the following scenario: a man sits in a coffee shop. He takes a seat and picks up the menu. After studying the menu for several minutes, the man carefully returns the menu to its placeholder before lighting a cigarette. A moment later, a waiter comes up to the man to take his order. The man looks at the waiter and nods hello. "May I have a vegetarian sandwich and a sweet coffee, please," the man says with a smile before adding, "Thank you."

Later, the same man returns to the same coffee shop. The man puts his feet up on the chair next to him. He then lights a cigarette and taps the ash onto the ground as he looks at the menu. He leaves the menu on the table as the waiter approaches. "Uh, bring me a vegetarian sandwich and a sweet coffee," he grunts, not even looking at the waiter. The man finishes by dropping his cigarette on the ground and crushing it under his shoe.

The two scenarios outlined above describe an

experiment carried out by researchers at the University of Amsterdam.[42] The aim of the experiment was to examine how people watching the experiment would react to the "polite man" in comparison to the "norm-violating man." The results of the study were both illuminating and insightful. People who viewed the footage of the man in the coffee shop rated the "polite man" as less powerful, whereas the "norm-violating man" was rated more powerful (even though the roles were played by the same actor). The implications of this study are both profound and instructive. The belief that you must be polite and kind to get ahead in life is nothing but an illusion. Women are attracted to men who project confidence and power. Bold men eat, while nice guys starve. To develop attraction, you must first develop the right mindset. You must be masculine. You must project strength. You must own your environment and your actions. And most important of all, you must be true to yourself and your desires.

PART TWO

CREATE ATTRACTION

*Nature is infinitely creative. It is always producing
the possibility of new beginnings.*

— Marianne Williamson

Attraction starts with a spark. You meet a woman,
and if she likes you and you seduce her the right way,
sex is all but guaranteed to happen. Only society has
drilled it into our heads that women don't want sex.
Women are pure creatures corrupted by man's lust.
This has a habit of making a man feel guilty for even
talking to a woman. Women are, however,
biologically programmed to want men to show
interest in them. That being said, before you think
about approaching and meeting women, it's
important to consider the role that logistics plays in
the seduction process. If your objective is to go out
into the world and meet beautiful women—location is
key. And just as a man who lives in a desert can't be a
fisherman, a man who lives in isolation will find it
difficult to meet, date, and seduce women.

If you're currently struggling to meet quality
women, it might be time to consider the importance
of location in your life. Simple logic dictates that men

who live in New York City have more dating options than men who live in Lost Springs, Wyoming (population 5). In the same way, men who teach English in Europe, Asia, or South America have more opportunities to meet, date, and have sex with women than men who work in a bank in a big metropolitan city. Meeting and dating women is not a question of resources, money, or prestige—it's simply a matter of access.

Men often believe that after college their glory days are over, as they find themselves falling into careers and lifestyles that severely limit their dating options. Yes, you might have a well-paid insurance job working forty hours a week, but your chance to meet, attract, and date beautiful women is going to be restricted by your lifestyle. Why do bartenders, tour guides, overseas English teachers, and personal trainers get to meet, date, and have sex with so many beautiful women? The answer is *access*.

As you read this, there are literally millions of women out there in the world who would be willing to date you and have an intimate relationship with you. This is no exaggeration. The only thing that prevents you from meeting these women is access. You can't date someone if you can't meet them. This is where the power of the direct approach, and to a lesser degree, online dating comes in. The ability to meet women is a crucial factor when it comes to dating success.

But not all locations offer the same opportunities. Take bars and clubs for example. If you walk into any club or bar and expect to meet beautiful women you won't be disappointed. You must be aware, however, that women enter clubs and bars with a certain mindset—that mindset is to have fun with their friends and try to attract as much attention from men as possible. To make matters worse, you not only have to compete with other men for a woman's attention, you also have to capture a woman's interest in a noisy, crowded environment. Nightclubs and bars are two of the worst places to meet and seduce women. Even if you exchange phone numbers, there's a good chance the woman will still flake on you. After all, the two of you just shared a fun drunken encounter and that's all it was. Somewhat counter-intuitively, some of the best opportunities to meet women can be had during the day when a woman's guard is down. You don't have to compete for her attention, and she doesn't have to worry about what her friends think as she tries to have a conversation with you over blaring music.

CASE STUDY #3: LOCATION IS KEY

Andrew lived with his parents in a small, quiet town in Florida. The town where Andrew lived was mostly full of retirees, and there was almost no way for Andrew to meet women unless he drove to one of the big cities nearby. Frustrated with his current living arrangement, Andrew decided it was time to move back to LA (where he went to college) or end up dying of sexual frustration.

A couple of months later, Andrew landed in LA, and as soon as he arrived he felt a sense of relief tinged with excitement. Everywhere he looked he saw beautiful women. It wasn't long, however, before Andrew realized that being surrounded by beautiful women wasn't going to improve his love life unless he could find a way to meet these women and talk to them.

After three months in LA, Andrew still hadn't met a girl he liked. If anything, he was feeling even more frustrated than before. The city wasn't the problem—he was surrounded by beautiful women every day. So, what exactly was going wrong for Andrew? In short, Andrew needed to learn one crucial skill: how to seduce women. Andrew was driving around LA, expecting women to just fall into his lap and that was never going to happen. Somehow, Andrew had to make his presence known. If he was going to have any success, Andrew would not only have to seek out and find attractive women, he would have to learn how to approach them and engage them in conversation.

⋏

Assuming you live in a town or city with a relatively large female population, you'll be able to meet women in the most unexpected locations. These locations include coffee shops, elevators, restaurants, concerts, supermarkets, the gym, parks, shops, malls, and just about any place that human beings congregate. Meeting women isn't difficult; meeting the right kind of women, however, requires more thought and attention. Yes, thousands of beautiful women can be found in bars and clubs, but as previously stated, bars and clubs aren't the most conducive environments for seduction. Instead, you must ask yourself what type of woman you want to meet?

It stands to reason, if you want to meet beautiful,

healthy women, you'll have a greater chance of success finding such a woman in the gym or a place where health-related activities take place. Interestingly enough, research has found that women who exercise or have just finished exercising, are much more likely to find a man attractive due to increased physiological arousal. Studies into exercise and attraction show that people are more likely to attribute an elevated heartbeat and feelings of arousal to the presence of a stranger as opposed to the actual source of their arousal—exercise.[43]

A similar well-known study was carried out on men over the Capilano River in North Vancouver, Canada. The researchers in the study had women approach men as they walked across a high suspension bridge. Afterwards, it was found that the men were more likely to find the women attractive when they were in a state of heightened physiological arousal.[44] In other words, the men confused fear, anxiety, and arousal for attraction. In the same way, if a woman's feeling fearful, anxious or aroused, she's more likely to be receptive to a man's advances, even if her arousal is triggered by something other than the man's presence.

The chaotic nature of life means you can only control so many variables at once. The opportunity to meet attractive women, however, is a variable that is largely out of your control. That's why it's so important to seize every opportunity you can to meet and interact with women whenever you get the chance. The man who pursues beautiful women ends up meeting and dating beautiful women. The man who settles for mediocrity ends up meeting and dating mediocre women. The choice, ultimately, lies with you. When it comes to meeting women who are worth pursuing, there are only two rules to keep in mind: first, it's easier to meet and seduce attractive women during the day; and second, you must be prepared to meet beautiful women in the most unexpected places without warning and without notice. This means you must be willing to act without hesitation or regret letting another opportunity pass you by.

APPROACHING WOMEN

Who dares wins.

— British SAS

Men who approach women directly have a rare
quality that women find intoxicating. These men have
nerve, confidence, and boldness—attributes that are
increasingly hard to find in the modern world. Men
who have the confidence to approach women directly
immediately set themselves apart from other men.
And although approaching women is often a nerve-
wracking experience, the rewards for having the
courage to toss rejection aside and go after what you
want inspires admiration and attraction in equal
measure.

Of course, most men prefer to take the safe
approach, opting to get to know a girl first before they
try to seduce her. As a man, however, it's always
better to state your intentions without fear of reprisal.
Yes, you can become friends with a woman, then try
to seduce her later on. Although this often leads to a
loss of attraction, as failure to take action and
approach women with boldness usually results in
metaphoric castration. But these are sensitive times
you tell yourself. What if she rejects me, or worse,
stops speaking to me? A woman will never hold it
against you for making your intentions clear and
expressing interest. Approach a woman with boldness

and it's unlikely she'll ever forget you. On the other hand, the man who waits for women to approach him in an almost catatonic, subdued state inspires neither interest nor attraction.

CASE STUDY #4: BOLDNESS INSPIRES ATTRACTION

Sabrina had only just broken up with her ex when she met Robbie online. The moment she started talking to Robbie, she felt an instant connection. When Sabrina finally got around to meeting Robbie, she was delighted to discover that she not only liked him online, she liked him even more in person. Robbie was fun to be around and the fact he was good looking only made him appear even more attractive. As the days went by, Sabrina and Robbie grew closer and closer. And the more time they spent together, the more they grew to like each other. It was now only a matter of time before they took their relationship to the next level.

* * *

One day as Sabrina was walking through the subway on her way to work, she heard an unfamiliar voice call out beside her—"I like your dress." Sabrina turned and saw a man standing beside her. "That's my favorite color."

"Really?" Sabrina laughed. "You like turquoise?"

"I love it."

"You don't think it's too bright?"

"It looks awesome."

"Thanks."

"My name's Paul by the way."

"Sabrina."

"Nice to meet you," Paul shook Sabrina's hand and continued to engage her in conversation. They chatted for a couple of minutes and Paul made no attempt to hide the fact that he was attracted to Sabrina. After all, why else would he stop and talk to her in the middle of the subway?

* * *

When Sabrina got home all she could think about was the confident stranger who'd asked for her number. It wasn't every day that a man approached her with such charm and confidence. Nowadays, it seemed that most men preferred to meet women online. Unfortunately for Robbie, he had no idea that in the space of an afternoon Sabrina's attraction for him had greatly diminished. Sabrina couldn't help it. Every time she thought about Paul, she smiled. Boy was he confident.

On the other hand, she had no way of knowing whether Robbie was confident or not. He was just some guy she had met online. What Paul did was something extraordinary—he had singled her out and made her feel special.

You can't seduce a woman if you don't talk to her. You might see an attractive woman in the park, but if you only look at her, you'll do nothing to establish a connection or build rapport. Your ability to connect with women on an emotional level allows you to take the interaction into the realm of the physical and beyond. Women crave emotional connection, yet many men are still too timid and apprehensive when it comes to opening up the channel of communication, waiting instead for that perfect moment. There is, of course, no such thing as a perfect moment. There are only opportunities—opportunities that are taken and opportunities that are missed.

CASE STUDY #5: MAKE YOUR INTENTIONS CLEAR

A group of international college students were staying in a hostel not far from the center of Rome. It was there, in the hostel, that the students met an Italian by the name of Paolo. Paolo was a modern-day Casanova, he loved women and he loved to flirt. The girls in the hostel, however, were already aware of Paolo's overly flirtatious behavior. And within the space of 24 hours, Paolo's reputation had been sullied and tarnished. Behind his back, the girls called Paolo a "creep" and a "pervert." After all, girls will be girls. But Paolo didn't care, he'd heard it all before. Instead, his attention was focused entirely on one girl and one girl only—Imogen.

"You're the most beautiful girl I've ever seen," Paolo said as he looked deep into Imogen's eyes.

"I want to kiss your beautiful lips," Imogen said as she told her friends what Paolo had said to her when she came back to the hostel.

"He said that? Oh, my God, what a creep."

"Weirdo, avoid," said Janice.

"So nasty."

"Ughhh," Imogen said. "Who does he think I am?"

As the girls sat around the hostel bar, having a good laugh at Paolo's expense, they were completely unaware that later that night, Imogen would end up sharing the same bed as Paolo. Paolo's bold, confident approach would ultimately prove too much for Imogen to resist. For as her friends sat around, talking about what a creep Paolo was, Imogen's imagination had started to run wild thinking about all the wonderful things Paolo might do to her. In a hostel full of horny young men and women, Paolo had been the only one who'd expressed any real interest in her. His romantic overtures made her feel alive. And although Imogen and her friends had been quick to dismiss Paolo and label him a "creep," Imogen knew her friends were just jealous because she was getting all the attention and they weren't. Paolo knew what he wanted and he knew a beautiful woman when he saw one. Ultimately, Paolo's direct approach was enough to secure a night of passion that Imogen would never forget.

⋏

A great approach is one of the most important elements of seduction. When a confident man approaches a woman, he makes her feel attractive and alive. And in the world of seduction, there's no greater aphrodisiac than confidence. As such, the direct approach is the strongest and most attractive form of introduction you can make. The confident man knows there's no such thing as a woman who's out of his league. A man with sufficient sexual market value can effectively pursue any woman no matter how attractive or unattainable she might appear to be—all that's required is the right approach.

APPROACH WOMEN NATURALLY

One of the most effective ways to approach women is to use an environmental approach. An environmental approach allows you to approach women using elements within the natural environment to make a woman feel more at ease. Imagine, for a moment, that you've just seen an attractive woman at the gym. You want to approach her, but you don't know what to say or how to break the ice. Using the environmental approach, there are literally thousands of things you can say to a woman in this situation. An example of an environmental approach in the gym would be to say: "Hey, how's your workout?" The same environment-specific approach can be used in the supermarket: "Hey, do you know where the [chocolate/milk/fish] is?"

Your approach doesn't have to be clever or entertaining. Instead, it's always better to talk to women as though you're talking to a close friend. Also, take note that women have a propensity to wear interesting trinkets and accessories. They style their hair in unique ways, sport tattoos, and color their nails. The next time you go out in public, take a moment to look at the women around you. What makes her stand out? What is it about her that catches your eye? Is it an item of clothing, her earrings, her hair, or even her shoes? All of these items are talking points that allow you to approach women in a natural and relaxed way. To give you an idea of how this works in practice, consider the following pickup lines as a great way to start a conversation:

— "Nice shoes."
— "I like your perfume."
— "That's a cool tattoo."
— "That bag looks heavy."
— "What are you drinking?"
— "That's my favorite color, I love [insert color]."

Simple, innocuous comments within the context of the woman's immediate environment work best here. There's no better way to signal outcome indifference and confidence than a light throwaway comment to disarm a woman and make her feel at ease. Remember, conversation is fluid as opposed to static. That's why it's always better to use an approach that can be adapted to your natural environment.

If you approach women in a positive, relaxed way, you communicate strength. But still the issue of what to say looms large. Trying to figure out what to say to a woman when you first meet her and what pickup lines work best is a question that's plagued men for decades. Now science can finally shed some much-needed insight into the conversation. One study published in the *Sex Roles* journal found that women prefer it when men approach them with a simple: "Hi" or "Hello."[45] Other effective pickup lines include the honest and direct: "Since we're both sitting alone, would you care to join me?" or "Do you want to dance?" Pickup lines such as: "Hey, what's your sign?" or "Did you hurt yourself when you fell from heaven?" were seen as less attractive, disingenuous ways to start a conversation.[46] That being said, you should simply use pickup lines as a way to assess whether or not a woman is interested in talking to you. Watch closely and you'll notice that a woman expresses all her intentions and desires through her actions. If a woman is open and interested in talking to you, she'll stop to engage you in conversation; if she isn't interested, she'll move away from you—it's that simple.

The moment you approach a woman, it's advisable to keep the conversation light and relaxed. Talk to her like you would talk to a close friend. There's no need to rush the interaction by trying to get intimate too soon. Yes, one night stands can and do happen, but usually only after a man has spent at least a couple of hours interacting with the woman first, even then a one night stand is never guaranteed.

One of the most famous studies in psychology, carried out on a college campus in the 1980s, proved that the odds of getting immediate sexual gratification from women was, surprisingly, not even 50 percent, but closer to zero percent.[47] In the study, attractive men and women were asked to approach complete strangers of the opposite sex, posing the question: "Would you go to bed with me tonight?" The results of the study showed that 70 percent of men agreed to the woman's request to go to bed with her that night. On the other hand, zero percent of women agreed to the man's request to have sex.

In case you think these findings are the result of a more conservative Anglo-Saxon culture, think again. The same study was replicated in sexually liberal France with exactly the same result.[48] Zero French women agreed to go to bed with a male stranger, even when the man was physically handsome. Women want sex just as much as men do, they just want it when they're ready and within the confines of a safe environment (drugs and alcohol notwithstanding).

CASE STUDY #6: BREAKING THE ICE

Simon saw the new waitress standing behind the counter as soon as he walked into the coffee shop. The moment he saw her, he was smitten. The waitress had long, flowing black hair and big brown puppy dog eyes. If I could marry a girl like that, I'd be happy for the rest of my life, Simon thought as he stepped up to the counter.

"What can I get you?" the waitress said, flashing a smile.

"Can I get a tall mochaccino please?"

"One tall mocha coming right up. Would you like anything else with that?" the waitress said.

For what felt like an eternity, Simon didn't know what to say. He looked at the waitress's nametag—*Christy*. He wanted to say something, anything, but his mind drew a blank. In the end, all he could muster was a simple, "Thanks, that's all."

"Here's your change," Christy said.

Simon looked at the waitress. He didn't want to leave, not yet. He wanted to say something funny or humorous, something that might impress her, but he couldn't think of anything smart enough or funny enough to say. Sensing an awkward silence, Simon stepped away from the counter and waited for his mochaccino to arrive.

Over the next couple of weeks, Simon became a

regular visitor at the coffee shop, coming almost every day to see Christy. But every time Simon ordered his coffee, he became increasingly frustrated by his own inability to get Christy to open up and talk to him.

* * *

The following week, Simon was in the coffee shop, having just ordered another mochaccino, when Derrick walked in. Derrick saw Christy standing behind the counter and liked what he saw straight away. As Derrick stepped up to the counter, he looked at the menu and noticed a wide selection of reserve coffee. Derrick paused for a moment, then turned to Christy and asked her what coffee she liked best. Christy let out a small, girlish giggle, and for the next five minutes, she spoke at length about all the different types of coffee they served. At one point, Derrick stopped Christy by touching her briefly on the arm to ask, "Where does your coffee come from." That's a dumb question, Simon thought as he listened in on their conversation. Christy laughed and told Derrick they sourced their coffee from Jamaica, Nicaragua, Kenya, Java, and Costa Rica—her favorite being Costa Rican coffee. Derrick smiled and told Christy, "I've never been to Costa Rica but I wouldn't mind a taste of it." Simon couldn't believe what he was hearing. He was furious. This guy had only just met Christy and now she was giggling and obviously having a great time talking to him. Life isn't fair, Simon thought as he walked out the door and threw his mochaccino in the trash.

A lot of men assume that women don't want to be approached and "hit on." This is true in so much that women don't want to be "hit on" in a crude or unflattering way. Women also don't want to be hit on by unattractive men. A woman will, of course, be flattered if a man with high sexual market value approaches her. As previously mentioned, women are biologically wired to receive men, they just want to be approached by the right kind of men.

Women live their lives in a waiting state. They wait for men to talk to them; they wait for men to approach them; and they wait for men to show interest, giving them the opportunity to either accept the man or reject him. A woman only resents it when a man shows interest in her if the man is weak, timid, or unattractive. You'll notice, however, that it's usually unattractive women who are the first to label men "creeps" and "perverts." How often do you see a beautiful woman at a feminist rally? It's the unattractive woman with low sexual market value who lashes out in anger and frustration. Her cries of feminism are, in reality, a cry for attention. A beautiful woman doesn't need to call attention to herself. For the most part, attractive women love men and enjoy their company. Their experience with society and men is usually a positive one. Feminine women respect the laws of nature and they understand that it's the man's role to approach her.

OVERCOME APPROACH ANXIETY

Approach anxiety is the amplified fear of rejection, and like all fears, it exists primarily within the confines of the mind. Approach anxiety can be so overwhelming it often induces paralysis in men. The most stifling aspect of approach anxiety is not knowing what to say. Take a moment, however, to imagine that your job involves approaching women. Every day you have to interview women for a survey about beauty products. You notice that your fear of rejection is greatly diminished when you approach women to fill out the survey. It doesn't matter whether women talk to you or not because they're not rejecting you personally, they're rejecting the survey. In this situation, it's easy to know what to say, and it's easy to move on to the next woman.

Now imagine you have to approach a woman because you want to get to know her in a more intimate way. You think about all the things you could say and you're instantly crippled by anxiety. What if she rejects me? What if she laughs at me? What if she humiliates me? And once more, your fear and anxiety stops you from approaching yet another beautiful woman.

CASE STUDY #7: ATTRACTION FAVORS THE BRAVE

Adam was having lunch with Josh when he noticed Josh making eye contact with someone behind him.

"What is it?" Adam asked.

"That girl keeps looking at me."

"Which girl?"

"The one sitting behind you."

Adam turned to see a beautiful girl sitting by herself at the table behind them. "Why don't you go talk to her," Adam said.

Josh shoveled a mouthful of pasta into his mouth. "Hmm, you think that's a good idea?"

"Sure, why not? She's obviously into you."

Josh looked doubtful. "I dunno, man. I wouldn't know what to say. Oh boy, she just looked over again. She's really cute."

"Dude, you gotta go talk to her, she likes you."

Josh looked down at his food. "Nah, she's probably not interested anyway."

"Trust me, if she looks at you and smiles, she's interested. She wants you to go and talk to her."

"Really?"

"Yeah."

"Could you do it for me? I mean, I really don't know what to say," Josh said.

"You sure?"

"Oh man, she just looked over again."

"Alright," Adam said. "But once I break the ice you better get your ass up there."

"You got it."

When the girl looked up again, she was surprised to see Adam, not Josh coming towards her.

"Hi," Adam said. "I hope I'm not disturbing you. My friend, he's a slow eater… he just asked me to come over and keep you company." Adam waved over at Josh. "I'm Adam by the way."

"Evelyn," the girl said with a tentative smile.

"Nice to meet you." Adam held out his hand and continued to engage Evelyn in conversation. A couple of minutes passed by before Josh finally finished his meal and came over to join them.

"He's right. I am a slow eater," Josh said as he rubbed his stomach.

Evelyn glanced at Josh, then turned her attention back to Adam. "You were saying?"

Despite Adam's best effort to include his friend in the conversation, Evelyn appeared to have lost all interest in Josh, even though he was the one who'd initially caught her eye. Her attention and interest was now focused entirely on Adam. As far as Evelyn was concerned, Josh was no longer a contender.

* * *

What happened? One minute, Evelyn was smiling and flirting with Josh, letting him know she found him attractive, practically inviting him to come over to speak to her. The next minute she was entirely focused on Adam. How could this happen? In one word: confidence. It was Adam, not Josh, who had the guts to go up and talk to her. It didn't matter that Josh was better looking, his hesitation communicated weakness. It was now too late to redeem the situation. The moment Josh allowed Adam to speak on his behalf was the moment Evelyn lost all attraction for him.

⋏

Missed opportunity hurts more than rejection. When your mind is flooded with doubt, it's important to remember that women want to be seduced. A woman might appear busy, filling her day with an endless array of activities. This doesn't change the fact that most women are starved for attention. A woman wants to live her life like it's a movie. A movie filled with drama, suspense, and romance. Her movie, however, is not of the gentle Disney variety. Her movie is much more brutish in nature. Women fantasize about being swept off their feet by a strong, confident man who's unable to resist her.

Keep in mind, no one is exempt from the daily grind of life, women included. Not even the most beautiful women are exempt from mundane tasks like sleeping, eating, working, and shopping. The sheer mind-numbing monotony of everyday life instills in women an insatiable desire for romance and passion. As a man, you must simply be aware of this desire. Women are constantly looking for stimulation and attention. If a woman believes your presence will bring passion and excitement into her life, she'll gladly receive you and welcome your approach. Keep in mind, women have evolved over thousands of years to respond to you as a man and find you attractive. The most natural thing in the world is for men and women to come together as one. In fact, you could argue that women desire this more than men because relationships are the centerpiece of a woman's life.

Women want you to take the initiative and start a conversation. You must revel in the fact that seduction is filled with anxiety and tension for the ability to overcome this anxiety is what separates you from other men. All seductions start with a spark—a spark that lights the fire of attraction. Whatever you want out of a relationship, whether it's a short-term fling, sex, or marriage, you must be able to approach a woman first to capture her attention and start the seduction process.

READ HER BODY

In the land of the blind, the one-eyed man is king.

— Erasmus

There is the misguided belief that the spoken word is the predominant form of communication among human beings when in fact there is another even more powerful form of communication that accounts for up to 60 to 80 percent of all communication. I am, of course, talking about body language. If only I could read a woman's mind and know what she's thinking, the frustrated man thinks as once more he's left rattled and confused by the actions of a woman he's trying to seduce. What's going on, he wonders. She tells me she likes me, but she never wants to see me.

Women communicate through body language and if you learn to read the signs you'll know when a woman is interested in you and you'll know when she's not. You'll also know when she's attracted to you and when it's time to make your move. Women have always used body language to communicate desire, men just have a difficult time reading the signals. Consider an interesting piece of research that found that women initiate up to 90 percent of all seductions.[49] Women do this in such a discreet way, however, that most men believe they're the ones making the first move.

CASE STUDY #8: A PICTURE TELLS A 1000 WORDS

Samantha was in a quiet hotel bar, drinking alone, when Bill came up and introduced himself. Bill, ever the gentleman, asked Samantha if he could sit down and buy her a drink. Throughout their entire conversation, Bill became increasingly flirtatious, often laying his hand on Samantha's shoulder whenever he made a point or told a joke. Bill was a natural conversationalist. He loved to tell stories and found it easy to make people laugh.

Sure enough, Samantha soon found herself laughing at just about everything Bill said. Bill had a feeling Samantha liked him, especially as she kept on telling him how funny he was. What Bill failed to notice, however, was the myriad of nonverbal cues Samantha kept sending his way. Despite the fact that Samantha was looking directly at Bill and smiling, her body told an entirely different story. The moment Bill sat down, Samantha grabbed her purse and crossed her arms. At no point during their conversation did she turn her body to face him. She even kept her legs crossed, pointing her feet away from him. As Bill continued to engage her in conversation, Samantha barely touched her drink and kept her wrists face down on the table. And even though Samantha continued to chitchat to Bill in a light-hearted way, not once did she touch her hair or touch her body to signal romantic interest. To the casual observer, Samantha's body language screamed *please leave me alone*. Bill, however, had no idea what Samantha was thinking because he was entirely focused on the sweet and encouraging words flowing from her mouth. Only when Bill finally asked Samantha for her phone number did he discover her true level of interest.

Fifteen minutes later, Bill skulked away from the bar, frustrated and humiliated. What a cock-tease, he thought. I bet she loves to lead men on. If only Bill knew how to read body language, he would have saved himself a lot of trouble and preserved his ego in the process.

ᚼ

In every seductive encounter, there's a natural process you must follow to build attraction before you can become intimate with a woman. Research into body language found that women use certain nonverbal cues to signal their interest and availability to men. These body language cues can be broken down into five distinct steps:

Step #1 (eye contact): The woman makes eye contact with the man, letting him know that she's noticed him. Once a woman makes eye contact with you, you're much more likely to get a positive response if you approach her.

Step #2 (smiling): Also referred to as the "invitation." The moment a woman smiles at you she's letting you know that she likes what she sees and she's inviting you to come and talk to her.

Step #3 (communication): A lot of researchers put step four, preening, before communication but in the vast majority of cases, the man talks to the woman right after she's made eye contact or smiled at him.

When you approach a woman before she's either seen you or smiled at you, you're playing a numbers game. In which case, you should immediately proceed to step four.

Step #4 (preening): This is the stage where a woman lets you know whether she's attracted to you or not. The woman preens herself to advertise her interest and encourage you to escalate the seduction. The following is a list of preening cues that women frequently use to signal sexual availability and interest:

— She blushes when talking
— She touches her neck and throat
— She frequently giggles and laughs
— Her breathing becomes deep and heavy
— She licks her lips, drawing attention to them
— She lets out a soft whimper or nervous laughter
— She points her body towards you, especially her knees and her feet
— She dangles her shoe from her foot, symbolizing the rhythm of sexual intercourse
— She reveals the underside of her wrist in a gesture of submission
— She strokes a phallic object (like her finger or a wine glass to let you know what she's really thinking)
— She plays with her hair and strokes it (one of the most common indicators of interest)
— She drops her gaze and looks at the ground in a gesture of submission

Step #5 (touch): The woman touches you to signal interest and to let you know that she's happy for you to take the interaction further.

In the same way that women use body language to signal interest, women also use body language to let men know when they're not interested in being seduced. It's important to understand what these nonverbal cues are so you can avoid wasting your time trying to seduce women who aren't interested. Closed, unreceptive body language is often displayed in one of the following ways:

— She crosses her legs and arms
— She keeps her wrists turned down
— She turns her feet and legs away from you
— She moves personal objects out of your reach
— She doesn't touch any objects or preen herself

When you pay close attention to a woman's body language, you'll quickly discover how a woman feels about you. You no longer have to try to figure out what she's thinking or feeling. The important thing to remember here is that female communication is covert as opposed to overt. A woman will rarely tell you that she likes you and wants to date you. This doesn't mean a woman won't signal her interest or availability. When a woman's attracted to you, she'll let you know by displaying, what are to her, obvious signs of interest.

Understanding how a woman communicates her interest is a crucial part of the seduction process. What does her body language tell you? Is her body language open or closed? Are her toes pointing towards you or away from you? A woman that's interested in you will make herself available to you. She'll communicate her interest through her body language and her actions.

Besides a woman's body language, there are even

more subtle signs of interest that you must be aware of. For instance, has the woman suddenly started wearing lipstick or perfume? Does she come and sit close to you? And does she frequent the same places you frequent? You only need be aware of such "coincidences" to realize that most women go out of their way to make themselves available to men they find attractive.

ATTRACTIVE BODY LANGUAGE

*The most important thing in communication
is hearing what isn't said.*

— Peter Drucker

Women by nature are more skilled at interpreting body language than men. A study conducted by Harvard University examined the difference between men and women when it came to reading a person's body language.[50] In the study, male and female participants were asked to view silent films of couples engaged in conversation. While watching the films, the participants were asked to interpret what was going on by studying the body language of couples in the film. The results of the experiment revealed that women were able to accurately interpret what was going on in the film 87 percent of the time, whereas men were only able to accurately interpret what was going on 42 percent of the time. These results appear to give women a significant advantage in the mating game as women are much more likely to be able to read a person's body language.

Further research into body language conducted by the University of Texas, Austin, noted that men are more likely to underestimate a woman's level of interest—although men looking for one night stands often overestimate a woman's sexual interest.[51] Conversely, the study found that most women underestimate a man's level of romantic interest. The findings of the study indicate that men are routinely selling themselves short. Not only do men frequently underestimate a woman's level of interest, but when they do show interest, women are unlikely to notice. The solution to this problem it seems is for men to be more direct in the way they communicate. Once you understand how to communicate desire, you will find that women become a lot more attracted to you in response. As the saying goes, first impressions count. And nonverbal communication is approximately 12 to 13 times more powerful than verbal communication.

Another illuminating piece of research found that more dominant and open power poses make men look more attractive.[52] When a man's body language is closed (for example, crossed arms or hunched shoulders), he is perceived as less attractive. The researchers in the study found that women were more likely to want to date someone with open and "expansive" body language. This means you must avoid making your body look small as though you're trying to hide from the world. There should be no hunched shoulders or crossed legs and arms, which displays a certain level of defensiveness and insecurity. You should also refrain from avoiding eye contact and looking at the ground in a gesture of submission.

Further research into attraction and body language conducted at Loyola Marymount University even went so far as to examine the effect that direct eye contact has on attraction.[53] The researchers came to the conclusion that men who looked a woman directly in the eye, especially while communicating, were perceived to be more intelligent, confident, and attractive than men who failed to maintain eye contact or only used limited eye contact.

At this point, it's worth noting that men who pretend to be someone they're not are easily red-flagged as pretenders. A study carried out by Queen's University found that sexual attraction is linked to the way men move their bodies.[54] Men who move in a natural, healthy, fluid way are more attractive compared to men who move unnaturally. As a general rule, it's always better to move naturally as opposed to moving in a way that you think will make you look more attractive.

Attempting to quantify the impact that body language has on attraction is no easy task. Nonverbal cues, however, are so powerful even the most casual observer can get a sense of a man's personality simply by watching the way he moves. A study carried out at Durham University showed a series of video clips of 26 students walking around campus.[55] Some of the students had loose, relaxed gaits, while other students had tighter gaits. After watching the students take only a couple of strides, the participants who viewed the footage rated the students with relaxed gaits as more confident, extrovert, adventurous, and attractive compared to those students who walked with tighter more "clipped" gaits that created the perception that the person was more neurotic, introverted, and unattractive.

One story that nicely demonstrates the power of body language is the famous casting of Sean Connery in the role of James Bond. When Connery walked in to audition for *Dr. No* (the first movie in the Bond franchise), the film's producers Albert R. Broccoli and

Harry Salzman, as well as the original author, Ian Flemming, had a more sophisticated character in mind for the role of Bond than the larger-framed Connery. Other big-name stars like Cary Grant, Michael Redgrave, and Richard Burton were being considered for the role, leaving Connery, a then relatively unknown actor, with little chance of getting the part.

Yat Malmgren, Sean Connery's acting coach at the time, explained how Connery had come to him only a couple of days before the audition. Connery told Malmgren that he would approach the audition by establishing himself as an "overpowering presence." During their discussion, Malmgren told Connery he should replicate the movements of a cat because "cats are loose and relaxed and languid."

On the day of the audition, Connery walked into the room, in Malmgren's words, "very self-assured, very large, and very secure." The producers instantly recognized star quality when they saw it. They knew without a doubt, after only a couple of seconds, that Connery had the masculinity and presence to play Bond. After the audition was over, the producers went to the window of their London office and watched as Connery sauntered like a panther down the sidewalk below. Brocolli would later recall, "It was the sheer self-confidence he exuded. I've never seen a surer guy... It wasn't just an act, either. When he left, we watched him through the window as he walked down the street. He walked like the most arrogant son-of-a-gun you've ever seen—as if he owned every bit of Jermyn Street from Regent Street to St James's. 'That's our Bond,' I said."[56]

The moment you demonstrate control over your environment and your body is the moment you command respect. One notable study showed that drivers, when parked behind a high-status car (such as a Porsche or Mercedes) at a set of traffic lights, were much less likely to honk their horn at the vehicle in front of them if the vehicle was high-status.[57] The explanation for this phenomenon is due to the level of respect high-status vehicles confer on their owners. People are more respectful and cautious around high-status people. In this particular experiment, the researchers drew the conclusion that if a person was driving an expensive car that person was more likely to be high-status. Furthermore, high-status people usually wield greater influence and power, and as a result, they're more likely to be able to retaliate and confront aggressors with a greater degree of force than the average citizen. Similarly, understanding how to project status and value through body language is an important skill to acquire. Open body language that demonstrates confidence and control over your environment is sure to leave a lasting impression on women.

EYES AND SMILES

*When a woman is talking to you, listen
to what she says with her eyes.*

— Victor Hugo

It's said that the eyes are the windows to the soul.
When a woman looks at you, even for just a brief
second, her look says a thousand words. When a
woman looks at you and gives you a coy smile, she is,
without doubt, expressing her interest and openly
inviting you to come and talk to her. Any approach
you make after a woman has made eye contact with
you will not only be welcomed, it will be expected.

A confident man knows how to use his eyes to catch
a woman's attention. When a woman looks deep into
your eyes, it's tempting to look away or be the first to
break eye contact. Resist this initial temptation to shift
your gaze elsewhere; instead, break the tension and
draw her in with a soft smile. Direct eye contact
without a smile is considered a threat and a challenge.
On the other hand, direct eye contact accompanied
by a smile or slightly raised eyebrows is seen as
charming and flirtatious. Don't worry about how a
woman will respond when you look directly into her
eyes and smile. Some women will smile back, letting
you know they're receptive to being approached. On
other occasions, when a woman doesn't return your
smile, don't allow yourself to become unsettled by her

apparent lack of interest. If your smile catches a woman by surprise, she won't have time to acknowledge you. It's only in the moment after you smile that she realizes what just happened. And if a woman likes you and is open to talking to you, expect her to look at you again—this time with a smile.

IS SMILING ATTRACTIVE TO WOMEN?

Studies into smiling and attractiveness show that women who smile are rated more attractive. But what do women think of men who smile? It's natural to assume that women are attracted to men who smile and appear friendly. Science, however, tells a different story. A study published in the journal *Emotion* found that women are more attracted to men who have brooding and mysterious facial expressions as opposed to men who have smiling, friendly expressions.[58]

In the study, the male and female participants were asked to rate the sexual attractiveness of members of the opposite sex when they displayed different facial expressions and emotions. These various facial expressions included happy (smiling), sad, moody, broody, proud, powerful, and confident expressions. What was most interesting about the study was that women rated the men who "smiled" as the least attractive. Men who displayed a "moody" appearance were rated more attractive than men in the "smiling" condition. Of all the different facial expressions, women rated the "broody" men as the most attractive. There are many reasons to explain these results. First, the man who smiles is more likely to be perceived as weak and open to influence and manipulation. A woman sees the man's smile for what it really is: an attempt on the part of the man to win favor by pretending to be nice. Conversely, the man who assumes a "broody" demeanor is more likely to appear masculine and less open to influence and manipulation.

At first, it's natural to assume that women would prefer being around men who are friendly and approachable, but the results of the study indicate that women are more likely to feel safe and secure around "broody" men because these men are more likely to be able to protect themselves and their loved ones in times of danger. By now you're probably wondering if it's ever okay to smile at a woman? And second, if you make eye contact, should you remain cold-faced and broody, or should you break the tension with a smile? The ideal strategy is to maintain a broody expression around women you want to seduce, then, when you make eye contact, you can offer the woman a muted impish smile to signal warmth and approachability. The impish smile is a slight smile that turns the edge of the mouth upwards then slides away just as easily as it appeared, projecting a look of bemusement as opposed to appearing overly excited by the woman's presence. At the same time, the impish smile allows you to maintain an aura of mystery as the woman is left wondering whether or not you actually like her.

Every time you smile at a stranger and use social graces like "please" and "thank you" you're attempting, either consciously or unconsciously, to ingratiate yourself with that person. When a man smiles for no reason, women become suspicious. The nice guy thinks that smiling at women will make him look more attractive. In reality, women are turned off by his all too familiar nice guy behavior. One study conducted by researchers at the University of British Colombia found that men are rated as less sexually attractive when they smile.[59] Even in online dating studies researchers found that men who posted pictures "not smiling" had more success compared to men who posted pictures of themselves "smiling." Any time you attempt to ingratiate yourself with a woman by smiling, you inadvertently run the risk of killing attraction.

One hallmark of the alpha male is that his thoughts and actions should be in perfect alignment. An alpha male smiles because he has a reason to smile, not because he feels socially compelled to do so. An alpha male is attractive because his emotions come from a place of honesty. The nice guy is anything but honest. The nice guy's actions are designed to please other people and do not reflect his true thoughts or feelings.

CASE STUDY #9: A SMILE IS ALL IT TAKES

Mike's birthday party was in full swing. And Larry had just arrived in time to see Mike blow out the candles on his birthday cake. As Mike was blowing out the candles, Larry noticed a beautiful woman standing in the crowd, singing "Happy Birthday."

An hour went by and Larry still couldn't take his eyes off the woman. Maybe it was the way her hair flowed down her back or the way her tight, green dress accentuated every curve on her body. Larry watched as the woman excused herself from a group of people and sauntered over to the poolside bar. This was the perfect opportunity to go and talk to her. Larry finished his beer and strolled over to the bar. Now would probably be a good time to say something, Larry thought as he ordered a whiskey on the rocks. And just as Larry was about to introduce himself, the woman turned and caught his eye. Larry flashed her a smile. "Hi," he said. "I'm Larry."

"Rachel," the woman replied.

"Are you friends with Mike?"

"Not a close friend, but I know him."

Larry and Rachel chatted for a couple of minutes before Rachel excused herself.

* * *

Rachel couldn't wait to get back to her friends. She had noticed Larry looking at her out the corner of her eye for the past hour and a half. That wasn't so bad, she was used to guys checking her out, but something about this guy was "off." First, there was the way he carried his drink with his arms folded across his chest. Then when he came over to the bar, she knew he was going to speak to her, but even then he looked nervous as he rubbed his face and scratched the back of his head.

* * *

Towards the end of the night, Larry saw a man walk up to Rachel and introduce himself. Rachel flashed the man a big, warm smile and the two of them were soon locked in conversation. Nothing to worry about, Larry thought. It's only Brad, Mike's friend from college. Whenever Larry saw Brad he rarely smiled or looked happy. He even looked bored as he stood there talking to Rachel. That's definitely nothing to worry about, Larry reassured himself. There's no way Rachel could fall for a broody, miserable guy like that.

* * *

Meanwhile, on the other side of the pool, Rachel couldn't take her eyes off Brad. She had noticed him about an hour ago when he first arrived, and something about the way he moved caught her attention. Maybe it was the way he strolled by the pool without a care in the world, his drink held loosely at his side with his jacket slung over his shoulder. Rachel couldn't understand what it was about him that she found so attractive. He wasn't that handsome, at least not in a conventional way, but there was something about him that drew her in. For one, he oozed confidence. He wasn't trying to fit in, he was just being himself. He appeared relaxed and mysterious all at the same time. Rachel felt attracted to Brad the moment she saw him. And when Brad finally introduced himself, Rachel knew she would find it difficult to resist this man. His presence was intoxicating.

The master seducer knows how to use his body to project an aura of strength and confidence at all times. He takes up space and maintains an expression that challenges people to impress him. He rarely if ever smiles, and when he does, it's a rare and precious gift. The skilled seducer strolls through the world at his own pace and never hurries or worries about a thing. His movements are akin to those of a cat—loose, relaxed, and languid. The world is there to serve him, not the other way around. It is this projection of attitude that makes the alpha male so irresistible and attractive to women.

ONLINE DATING

The goal of online dating is to get
offline as fast as possible.

— Ruth Webb

One of the main advantages of online dating is that it allows men to connect with hundreds of women in a relatively short space of time. At no other time in history has it been easier to connect with so many women so quickly. A man with low self-esteem and almost no confidence can now interact with more women in a single week than Casanova could expect to meet in his entire life. Having unlimited access to women, however, doesn't make the seduction process any easier.

Before the birth of the Internet, a man had to go out and seduce women face-to-face. He either failed in this endeavor or succeeded. In previous generations, if you wanted to meet a woman and become intimate with her, you had to summon a degree of courage to make this happen. The Internet erases the initial fear and anxiety that comes with meeting women for the first time. After all, how scary is it to talk to someone online? And how scary is it to talk to someone who's made it abundantly clear that they too are also looking for romance and intimacy? Despite this, you mustn't be lulled into thinking that online dating is a problem free zone. There are, as you're about to discover, many problems to overcome when it comes to online dating.

When you meet women online, you bypass an important part of the seduction process—the direct approach, a chance to display confidence and strength. As a result, anytime you meet a woman online, a woman is going to have lower levels of attraction for you than she would have if she had met you in person as one question remains to be answered: are you capable of seducing her without the help of the Internet? To answer this question, a woman will undoubtedly test you to get a true measure of your strength.

In the world of online dating, you're judged first and foremost by your appearance. If you're to have any success developing attraction online, you must first learn to cultivate an attractive image. You can achieve this by posting pictures that portray you in a strong, positive light. Indeed, first impressions are so powerful, research published in the *Personality & Social Psychology Bulletin* discovered that people can accurately predict the personality of people they see for the first time, even in photographs.[60] Qualities like extraversion, self-esteem, confidence, health, and emotional stability can all be judged accurately simply by looking at a person's appearance.

CASE STUDY #10: APPEARANCES ARE EVERYTHING

Vanessa broke up with her ex around six months ago, and only now, after going through a lot of emotional turmoil, did she feel ready to dip her toes into the water and start dating again. Her friends were all dating men they'd met online, and Vanessa thought the Internet would be a good place to start. That was how she met Carl. After being online for only a couple of days, Vanessa saw Carl's profile and was instantly impressed. Carl looked confident and sophisticated. And when they got around to chatting online, Vanessa found him easy to talk to.

When Vanessa met Carl in person, however, she was instantly disappointed. Where was the confident man she had met online? In the flesh, Carl was neither funny nor charming. He was clearly out of shape, something his profile pictures did well to conceal, and his elegant turn of phrase had been replaced by the rambling stutter of a man who was insecure around women. Even though Vanessa was attracted to Carl online, her impression of him now was nothing short of disappointing.

⋏

It doesn't matter how attractive your online profile is and how well you communicate, if a woman isn't attracted to you in person, there's nothing you can do to redeem the situation. One of the great perils of online dating is the speed with which a man and a woman can become intimate in such a short space of time; although this intimacy is often an illusion, as the woman soon discovers that the "online" version of the man is nothing like the "real" version.

Even if you're confident and attractive, there's still another problem that must be overcome. When you become intimate with a woman online without first meeting her in person, you unconsciously derail the seduction process. Men often lament how they "talked to a girl for hours" or how "they became so close online they both agreed not to meet and date other people." Unfortunately, theirs was a relationship built on nothing more than hope and illusion. It's only when you sit down face-to-face that the real seduction begins.

USE SOCIAL MEDIA TO YOUR ADVANTAGE

Appearance rules the world.

— Frederick Schiller

Used the right way, social media can stimulate attraction and build intrigue; used the wrong way, however, and social media has the potential to wreak havoc and make you look desperate and weak. It's for this reason that we must examine social media—not just as a way to build attraction, but also as a way to avoid killing attraction altogether. The dark side of social media is that so much of it is ego driven. When a woman posts a picture of herself online, men often assume that the best way to get her attention is to start liking all her posts and pictures in return. In other words, they inadvertently become just another "fanboy."

A surprising number of men believe they can capture a woman's interest by liking all her social media updates. If building attraction were that easy, every man would be having sex with the girl of his dreams. That's not to say liking a woman's posts doesn't have its place. Intermittently liking a woman's posts lets her know that you're aware of her presence and that you might be interested in her—*might* being the operative word here for doubt and uncertainty are key factors when it comes to building attraction.

CASE STUDY #11: THE DANGERS OF SOCIAL MEDIA

When Laura found Jordan's profile on social media, she couldn't believe it—Jordan had changed so much, she hardly recognized him. In high school, Jordan had been a skinny, little kid; now he was a strong, handsome man. After exchanging a couple of messages, Laura and Jordan both agreed they should meet up in person. It wasn't long, however, before Laura found herself getting turned off by Jordan's behavior. Every time she posted a picture or comment, Jordan would always like it. It didn't matter what she posted, Jordan would always comment or like her post straight away. Laura didn't know why, but she began to feel like she was losing interest in Jordan. Why was he so responsive to everything she did? His availability and high level of interest reeked of desperation.

When Jordan tried to meet up with Laura the following weekend, Laura told him she was busy and would be unavailable for the next couple of weeks. And although Jordan was frustrated by Laura's response, it didn't stop him from liking all her posts and updates on social media. Jordan believed that if he continued to shower Laura with enough attention, she would soon come to realize what an amazing guy he was.

What Jordan didn't know was that Laura had also been checking out the profile of another guy she'd met a couple of weeks ago (some guy called Nick). Nick wasn't that active on social media, but whenever he did post a photo or comment, he was always doing something fun and interesting. Usually, he was taking a trip, riding his bike, or going scuba diving. The more Laura looked at Nick's profile, the more she liked him.

Over the next couple of weeks, Laura found herself thinking more and more about Nick. What kind of man was he? She had no idea. He only occasionally liked her posts and he only messaged her if she reached out and messaged him first. Nick was a complete mystery. But from what Laura could see, he was definitely a fun and attractive guy to be around. Maybe I should send him a message and ask him out on a date, Laura thought.

ʎ

Researchers at the University of Alaska found that women are more attracted to men who take "hunter-gatherer" type risks as opposed to stupid risks.[61] Hunter-gatherer type risks include outdoor physical activities like mountain biking, scuba diving, rock climbing, and extreme sports. The results of the study found that women are more attracted to men who take risks similar to those faced by our hunter-gatherer ancestors. In contrast, men who performed what were considered "stupid risks" were found to be significantly less attractive. A good example of a stupid risk would be handling dangerous chemicals in an unsafe way, plagiarizing an academic paper, or stealing.

Additional research published in *CyberPsychology &*

Behavior revealed that social media is also most likely responsible for increased levels of jealousy and suspicion in relationships.[62] Because the nature of social media is often ambiguous and open to interpretation, it often leads to high levels of jealousy amongst both men and women. This knowledge, of course, can be used to your advantage.

Creating artificial jealousy is often an effective way to capture a woman's attention and restore fading interest. If you want to introduce the element of jealousy into your relationship, however, you must refrain from being too overt and direct. Posting pictures on social media of yourself being intimate with another woman will only instill resentment and throw up more problems and resistance. Instead, it's better to be seen pictured with attractive women as opposed to being intimate with them. One picture with an attractive woman is all you need to create a sense of anxiety and discomfort. A woman's mind will naturally gravitate towards feelings of jealousy, which, in turn, will lead her to feel heightened levels of attraction for you.

It's also worth noting that researchers at Texas Christian University discovered that women find men more attractive when the man is pictured with other attractive women (this can include attractive ex-girlfriends and even strangers).[63] This phenomenon, known as *mate choice copying*, builds on the theory that men become more attractive when they're chosen by other attractive women. And even though attraction, in this case, is based on nothing more than a mental shortcut, the impact of mate choice copying on attraction mustn't be overlooked.

If your goal is to build attraction, you should post as many high-status pictures on social media as possible. A study published in the *British Journal of Psychology* brought to light an interesting aspect of attraction.[64] The study revealed that men who posted pictures of themselves sitting in a Bentley Continental were immediately seen as more attractive than men pictured in a Ford Fiesta. Okay, no real surprise there. Yet another study published in the *Journal of Evolutionary Psychology* found that men who had their picture taken inside a luxury apartment were rated more attractive than the same men pictured outside on the street.[65] Women by nature are attracted to high-value men. The expensive car, the luxury apartment, the lavish lifestyle all indicate that a man is likely to possess high-value traits such as confidence, intelligence, strength, and persistence.

You mustn't assume that you have to rely solely on ostentatious displays of wealth to build attraction on social media. You only need to make sure that the pictures you post reflect a lifestyle that's both appealing and attractive. Pictures of physical activity, traveling, developing a business, and working on a hobby are all pictures that communicate high-value. Another study that explored the effect of social proof on attraction was carried out by researchers at the University of California at San Diego.[66] The study found that men and women usually look better when photographed as part of a group.

When it comes to creating attraction, everything you post online should be geared towards building value and status. Because human beings are social creatures, you mustn't forget the power of *social proof* and the role it plays in attraction. One excellent form of social proof is *preselection*. So how exactly does preselection work?

A man walks into a bar by himself. The women in the bar look at the man and think nothing of it—all they see is a man walking into the bar, he could be anyone. Now imagine the same man walks into the same bar and this time he has a beautiful woman on his arm. The other women see the man and their reaction is now completely different. The man is no longer just a regular guy who walked in off the street. What is it about this man that enabled him to attract such a beautiful woman into his life? This is the power of social proof. The man has already been preselected by a beautiful woman, the other women in the bar see this and automatically assume the man has high-value.

In a similar way, when you walk past a restaurant and see a crowd of people lined up outside, you are naturally inclined to wonder what's so special about that restaurant in particular. Most people will assume the food is exceptional because so many people want to eat there. This, once again, is the power of social proof. The Royal Society published an interesting study that helps to explain the power of social proof in more detail. The study analyzed how female participants would react to different pictures of a man and woman (with the woman looking at the man with different facial expressions).[67] In the pictures, the woman's facial expressions were either (a) smiling (b) bored, or (c) neutral. The results of the study showed that the female participants rated the man most attractive in those pictures where the woman was seen "smiling" at the man.

Other studies evaluating the effect of social proof on attraction found similar results. One such study published in the *Journal of Social, Evolutionary and Cultural Psychology* explained how women are more likely to be drawn to men who are already in a relationship, as opposed to men who are single.[68] Further research into this dark area of attraction revealed that women only find men attractive in this situation if the man is dating an attractive woman. In other words, if you're seen walking around with plain Jane, you'll do nothing to inspire interest or raise your value.[69]

Social proof can be used to great effect on social media. And based on the body of scientific research that already exists in this field, it's safe to say that men who are seen with attractive women immediately raise their value and become more attractive as a result. Any time you raise your value to the point where you've acquired a certain level of prestige and recognition (for example, you're seen with a beautiful woman, you're a semi-celebrity, or you've achieved recognition in a particular field or industry), you exhibit social proof and value.

Even when you're simply having a good time, hanging out with a group of friends, you have an opportunity to display positive social proof based on the fact that you're socially aware and liked by your peers. Displaying social proof is a great way to build attraction for human beings are nothing if not social animals.

TEXTING AND CALLING

I think what ruins relationships and causes most fights is insecurity.

— Oscar Wilde

You live in an age where you can now contact a woman anytime, day or night, without restriction, and without difficulty. In the history of mankind, this has never before been possible—until now. Our ability to communicate 24/7 has made the dating game a whole lot easier, yet it's also brought with it a whole new set of problems. The first problem is that women no longer exclusively use the phone as a way to communicate, the phone is now frequently used as a psychological weapon. At no other time in history has it been easier for women to test men and wreak havoc on their emotions. Women know that if they can unsettle a man, there's a good chance they'll be able to expose his insecurities and find out just how confident he really is. This is why it's so important to understand how to text and call a woman the right way.

Ninety-five percent of men get a woman's contact details and immediately ask the woman out on a date. Yes, you want to ask her out, but not with your first message. The first message you send to a woman should simply be a "feeler message." At this point, all you're trying to do is figure out if the woman is interested in you or not. Your first message to a woman should be something simple along the lines of: *"Hey, it was nice to meet you."* Nothing more, nothing less. You're not enquiring into how she's doing or appearing too interested at this point. As always, it's important to cultivate an aura of mystery and suspense.

Most men remain ignorant of the fact that longer messages only make them look more responsive and thus more desperate. This does nothing to raise a woman's attraction or cultivate an aura of mystery. The same applies to talking on the phone for hours on end. As with all areas of seduction, less is more. There are, after all, only so many things you can say to a woman before she knows everything about you. If you try to get too close to a woman too soon, you run the risk of giving away too much information. You become a known quantity; and while this brings with it the elements of safety and security, it does nothing to build a sense of intrigue and fascination.

If a woman is interested in you, she'll be in touch. You don't raise a woman's attraction by sending her lots of messages and calling her on the phone. To get a sense of whether a woman is interested in seeing you or not, all you have to do is send her one message and wait for her to respond. No response means she's either not interested or she's seeing someone else. If you receive no reply from your initial message, there's no point sending another message in a desperate attempt to try and win her over.

Only when a woman responds to your initial message, should you respond with some light-hearted banter before using this as an opportunity to ask her out on a date. If, for whatever reason, a woman is unable to meet up with you, it's important to remain unaffected by her response. She might be genuinely busy and unable to meet you even if she wants to. It is, however, easy to kill attraction by handling resistance the wrong way. You might interpret a woman's initial resistance as a sign of rejection. This is the moment most men become hyper-responsive, bombarding women with messages and phone calls without waiting for a response.

The rules of attraction dictate that you should never display too much interest in a woman too soon to preserve your value and create an aura of mystery. One sure way to kill attraction is to send too many messages without giving a woman enough time to respond. It's essential that you allow a woman the opportunity reach out to you after you send her a message. The natural flow of a text conversation should resemble that of a face-to-face conversation. In face-to-face conversation, a speaker who rambles without letting the other person speak comes across as overbearing and tiresome.

If you send too many messages without giving a woman the chance to respond, you're telling the woman that you want her more than she wants you, and that's never a good foundation for attraction. Consider the following text conversation between Stan and Diane:

Stan: *Hey Di, it was great to meet you the other day. How are you?*

(No response from Diane.)

Stan: *Just finished work. Now on my way to the gym :)*

Stan: *What are you up to this evening?*

Diane: *Hey, super busy day. Need to workout myself.*

Stan: *Hope you have a great workout. What kind of workout are you doing?*

Stan: *I just did some weights and cardio.*

Stan: *Need to bust my stress. My day was crazy busy too!*

(No response from Diane.)

Stan: *Let me know if you'd like to catch up over the weekend. If you're free? :)*

In this situation, Diane might have been legitimately busy or she might have been testing Stan. Either way, Stan failed to give Diane enough time to respond. By sending seven messages to Diane's one solitary message, Stan displayed a weak, insecure side of himself that did nothing but lower Diane's attraction for him.

In the early stages of the relationship, it's easy to fall into the trap of texting a woman for hours on end. Resist this trap, for it offers few rewards. You might feel an intense level of desire and comfort when you speak to a woman. You might feel the need to express this desire when you communicate, convinced that doing so will bring the two of you closer together and strengthen the bond between you. Many good men have fallen into this trap with disastrous consequences.

A study published in *Psychological Science* examined how women reacted to men who expressed different types of feelings for them.[70] In the study, the women were asked to rate men in three different categories. In the first category, the women were told the men "liked" them. In the second category, the women were told the men had "no feelings" for them. And in the third category, the women were told it was "unknown" how the men felt about them. What was interesting about this study was that the women didn't rate the men who "liked" them as the most attractive; surprisingly, the women rated the men whose feelings for them were "unknown" as the most attractive. The study also revealed that the women found themselves thinking most often about the men whose feelings were "unknown" as opposed to the men who "liked" them or had "no feelings" for them at all. This study demonstrates that uncertainty increases a woman's attraction for a man. There's no doubt the more a woman thinks about you, the more likely she is to find you attractive and desirable.

Equally interesting research published in the *Journal of Experimental Social Psychology* examined the power of winning a lover over.[71] The participants in the study were asked to engage in a series of meetings. During these meetings, each participant would "accidentally" overhear one of the experimenters describe the participant in one of four ways: (1) all positive: (2) all negative; (3) initially negative but becoming positive; or (4) initially positive but becoming negative. It was predicted that the participants in the study would like the experimenter more when the experimenter's assessment of them was "all positive." What the researchers discovered, however, was that the participants in the study liked the experimenter more when the experimenter's assessment of them was "initially negative but becoming positive." The findings of this study can just as easily apply to the world of dating, where a woman is much more likely to find you desirable and attractive if she has to win you over as opposed to knowing that you liked her right from the start.

CASE STUDY #12: BE A CHALLENGE

Greg was attracted to Michelle the moment he saw her running on the treadmill at the gym. After summoning the courage to ask her out, Greg and Michelle soon started dating. Greg couldn't believe his luck. Here was a woman who was not only beautiful and smart, she was also in great shape and had a body to die for.

Greg and Michelle had now been dating for three months, and the more time they spent together, the more they liked each other. Greg had dated a lot of women in the past, but Michelle stood head and shoulders above the rest. Now, in his early forties, Greg was looking to settle down and start a family.

Every morning, Greg would start the day by sending Michelle a message telling her how much he loved her and cared about her. Michelle loved this. Greg was sweet, attractive, successful, and kind. In fact, he was just about the kindest man Michelle had ever met. It was nice to feel loved and appreciated for once, especially after having had so many bad relationships in the past.

Michelle loved how she could talk to Greg on the phone for hours, talking about anything and everything. That is until one morning Greg sent Michelle another *"Rise and shine, I love you"* message. For the first time in their relationship, Michelle no longer felt the need to respond. She couldn't explain why she felt this way. When Michelle looked at Greg's message, she felt nothing. No need to panic, Michelle thought as she fired off a quick *"Love you too"* in response. Greg had no idea that endlessly expressing his love and devotion had slowly but surely killed Michelle's attraction for him.

⚔

Talking too long on the phone, sending too many messages, initiating every conversation, and expressing your love and devotion are all common traps that men fall into. If your goal is to raise a woman's attraction, you must learn to project strength and value even when speaking and texting on the phone. And although it's your role as a man to initiate and chase a woman at the beginning of the relationship, this doesn't mean you should send a woman a stream of messages if she doesn't respond to you. All you have to do is send one message, then give her enough time to respond. Whether it takes her a minute to get back to you or a week is immaterial.

There will always be times when a woman goes cold and she decides to ignore a man's messages. The woman might be genuinely busy, she might be in a bad mood, or she might be testing you. Whatever the reason, you must wait for a woman to respond in her own time, even if this means walking away until she gets back to you. If a woman takes an hour to respond, simply mirror her response time. If she responds within five minutes, feel free to respond in a similar timeframe. If a woman doesn't get back to you for a day or two, return the favor and respond the following day. Don't feel as though you have to respond straight away just because it's the "nice" thing to do. And don't be afraid to make her wait. Just because it's polite doesn't mean it's right.

CASE STUDY #13: EXPOSING INSECURITIES

Kyle didn't try to hide the fact that he was falling head-over-heels in love with Anita. She was the sexiest girl he had ever dated; not only that, she was easy-going and even easier to talk to. During the week, when Kyle and Anita didn't see each other, they would often spend hours talking to each other on the phone.

One afternoon, Kyle sent Anita a message: *"Hey, how's your day going?"* Four hours later, Kyle was still waiting for Anita to respond. What's going on? Kyle thought. Has she lost interest in me? Kyle decided to send Anita another message to find out what was going on.

* * *

Anita was driving to the gym when she saw Kyle's message. She couldn't respond right there and then so she told herself she would get back to him when she wasn't driving. Anita drove to the gym then went to the supermarket. It was a busy afternoon and she kept telling herself to send Kyle a message as soon as she got home. When Anita got home three hours later, she was exhausted and decided to jump in the shower then grab something to eat. She reminded herself to call Kyle right after she finished dinner. When Anita eventually got around to checking her phone, she saw a bunch of missed calls and messages from Kyle.

Kyle: *Hey, I guess you've been really busy this afternoon. What are you doing?*

Kyle: *Just going out for dinner, want to join me?*

Kyle: *Is everything okay?*

Kyle: *What's going on? Has something happened?*
Kyle: *Where are you?*

Anita sighed with disappointment. She thought back to a time when she had dated a guy called Will. Once, when she didn't respond to Will for half a day, she remembered how he had gone crazy and proceeded to blow-up her phone. Without even realizing it, Kyle had just made a similar mistake. All those messages seeking reassurance exposed a weakness Anita had seen before in her ex-boyfriend, and she wouldn't hesitate to dump Kyle if he acted the same way.

⋏

Attraction grows in space, not in close proximity. If you want to raise a woman's attraction for you, you first need to get her thinking about you. Being less responsive is one way to accomplish this. There's a deep underlying psychology when it comes to texting and calling women if you want to build attraction. What you say, how you say it, how long your messages are, how frequently you send messages, who initiates first, and how fast you respond communicates either weakness or strength. When a man immediately responds to a woman's messages, the woman can't help but feel the man's desperation. And what kind of man is desperate? The weak and unattractive man.

Numerous psychological studies show that men who are highly responsive are less attractive to women. A responsive behavior set is comprised of behaviors that signal that a man "understands, values, and is willing to support a woman and invest his resources into the relationship." In other words, he is prepared to become the ultimate provider both physically and emotionally.[72] Most men believe that acting this way is a good thing. They assume the more supportive, understanding, and responsive they are the more likely a woman is to find them attractive. And while it's true that men find responsive women attractive, women don't feel the same way about responsive men.

If there are any lessons to be learned from studies into attraction, it's that women aren't attracted to nice guys. They're attracted to men who project strength and confidence. If you start with the fundamental truth that women are attracted to strength in all its various forms and guises, it becomes a lot easier to see why being a "nice guy" and why being responsive is so unattractive. From a woman's perspective, a responsive man is more likely to be exploited by others. The responsive man also sends the signal that he's eager to please, has a weaker character, and has fewer dating options.[73]

If you're over responsive and too available, you communicate weakness. A woman wants to know that she can have space without having to worry about you getting upset or becoming clingy. Every human being wants freedom. If a woman thinks you'll try to restrict her freedom in any way, she'll instinctively pull away from you. It's only in times of strife and uncertainty that problems arise. You must never allow your fears and insecurities to derail what should otherwise be a straightforward seduction. With this in mind, you must be conscious of where you stand in the seduction process and how fast you respond to women.

When a woman sends you messages, you must be acutely aware of how long her messages are, and also how long your messages are in response. If a woman sends you short, abrupt messages, her current level of attraction for you is low. Never make the mistake of responding to short messages with an overly long response. If, for whatever reason, a woman sends you short messages, which indicate a severe lack of interest, simply delay your response time, replicating a similar lack of interest. Alternatively, sending no message at all is often the perfect way to allow a sense of anxiety to creep into the woman's mind and grab her attention. One of the main drawbacks to modern technology is that it's now easier than ever for women to test men. Be aware that technology can be used to project strength and it can also be used to expose weakness—which response will you choose?

SETTING DATES

Genius is patience.

— Isaac Newton

If a woman is attracted to you and wants to see you, setting a date to meet in person is easy. Logistics, however, are a significant part of the seduction process. Yet the importance of logistics is often overlooked. It doesn't matter if a woman is attracted to you or not, if she can't see you because you live too far away, or because your work schedule conflicts with her work schedule, it will be impossible to take the seduction to the next level.

FIRST DATES

If you live relatively close to a woman, meeting up during a weekday evening is often the most convenient and least threatening time to meet up. In this situation, it's always better to push for a date on a weekday evening, which comes with a natural time constraint built in, as opposed to a weekend date, which carries with it the weight of expectation. A woman's weekend is often reserved for close friends and family.

If a woman lives far away, you'll have no choice but to see her on the weekend. In this situation, there's no point sending a woman a message early on in the week, trying to set a date for the weekend. Instead, you must give her time to think about you. If you're too available, you become boring and predictable. The unattractive man, in a moment of desperation, rushes to set a date, scaring the woman away in the process. The skilled seducer, on the other hand, isn't afraid to wait and bide his time for the perfect moment. He understands that waiting will prime a woman and make her even more excited to see him.

FOLLOW-UP DATES

After you've had one or two successful dates with a woman, don't be in a rush to see her again too soon. Patience is a virtue. You must give a woman time to miss you. As a man, it's natural to want immediate gratification. We want to have sex as fast as possible. We want love and affection straight away. In short, we want to have our cake and eat it. Nonetheless, if you rush the seduction process you're telling a woman that you don't have control over yourself and your emotions.

The seduction process is, in many ways, like going fishing. You hook a fish and the fish starts to struggle. The more the fish struggles, the more tired it gets. You now have an opportunity to land the fish, but you must be careful. If you're impatient at this point, there's a good chance you'll snap the line and the fish will get away. As you draw the fish closer, you must remember to occasionally let the line go slack and allow the fish to pull away from you. Women are in many ways similar to fish. If you try to draw a woman in too soon, there's a good chance you'll scare her away. You must allow a woman to pull away from you, then come back when she's ready. If you try to set a date too soon, you risk snapping the line and losing the woman forever.

WHEN SHE FLAKES AND CANCELS DATES

There are no desperate situations,
only desperate people.

— Heinz Guderian

There's nothing more frustrating than having a date setup only for a woman to flake and cancel at the last minute. To better understand why women flake and cancel dates, it's important to get inside a woman's head and understand the female mindset. When a man meets a woman for the first time, he's usually struck by the visual. He's intoxicated by the woman's appearance and can't stop thinking about her. The same, however, cannot be said of women. When a woman and man meet for the first time, the man is instantly attracted to the woman and curious to get to know more about her. The woman is also curious about the man too and would like to get to know more about him, but not with the same speed and level of intensity.

Before they part ways, the man and woman exchange numbers and express a mutual desire to meet up in the not too distant future. The man goes home and starts to think obsessively about the woman, wondering if he'll ever see her again. The man is driven, first and foremost, by his biological need to have sex. This life force, or sexual energy, is what drives a man to go out into the world to meet, date, and have sex with women. In contrast, women aren't propelled by the same life force to go out into the world and have sex in the same way that men are. This is why it's so much easier for women to be patient in the early stages of a relationship. Before we look at how to handle flaky behavior, it's important to examine the main reasons why women flake and cancel dates.

SHE'S NOT FEELING IT

She might be having a bad day. She might have had an argument with her best friend. She might be feeling stressed out from work. It's not that the woman wasn't feeling good vibes about you, or that she won't feel good vibes about you in the future, but right now, she isn't in the mood to see you or anyone else for that matter. That's not to say she won't change her mind. A woman's emotions are never static, and her mood can easily change from happy to sad and back again all within the space of an hour.

SHE'S IN LOVE WITH SOMEONE ELSE

Yes, a woman might give you her phone number and flirt with you even if she's already in a relationship with someone else. She might even be flattered by your attention. That doesn't mean to say that she's open to dating you and taking things further. If a woman's already in love with someone else, nothing you do or say will convince her to throw her current relationship away.

SHE'S LOOKING FOR VALIDATION

Women love getting validation from men because it feeds their ego and makes them feel sexy and beautiful. The man who engages in extended online/phone conversations that lead nowhere does nothing but feed a woman's ego and desire for validation. A woman might give you her contact details, not because she's interested in having a relationship with you, but because she wants to feel validated and desired. Your interest makes her feel attractive, that's all.

SHE HAS A GENUINE REASON

If a woman is on her period, is sick, is under a deadline, or another unexpected problem has occurred, don't be surprised if she flakes on you. It's not that she doesn't want to see you, she does. She just has a genuine reason why she can't see you right now. If a woman genuinely wants to see you, she'll get back to you and let you know when she's available at another time and date that's more convenient.

SHE'S TESTING YOU

When a woman tests you, she's looking for visible signs of weakness. Flaking is an easy way to test men for weakness because flaking usually elicits an emotional response, causing most men to respond with anger, frustration, or panic. This tells the woman that the man is overly invested in her before he's even got to know her. This is a red flag to women. When a woman's testing you, it's important to remain calm and unaffected by a woman's flaky behavior. Expect women to flake and don't be surprised when it happens.

CASE STUDY #14: FLAKY BEHAVIOR

Miguel was at a bar with some friends when he accidentally knocked into Mary. Instead of getting angry, Mary smiled and playfully punched Miguel on the arm. Miguel insisted on buying Mary a drink and they hit it off straight away. For the next two hours, Miguel and Mary stood in a corner of the bar, talking about everything from music to sport. After that night, Miguel was hooked. He couldn't stop thinking about Mary. Their attraction was so strong, they both agreed they should catch up over the weekend.

On Friday morning, Miguel sent Mary a message to make sure their date was still on. When Mary got back to Miguel, however, it wasn't the kind of message he was expecting. Miguel blinked several times as he re-read Mary's message: *"Hey, I'm really sorry, but I don't think I can make it this weekend. Got so many things to catch up on."*

Miguel felt a surge of anger and frustration. He squeezed his phone, then typed out a reply, trying his best to stay calm: *"No problem. Let's catch up this evening."*

"I'm really sorry. I can't this weekend. Maybe next week,"

Mary replied.

Miguel's blood began to boil. He had seen flaky behavior before and he wasn't going to let Mary disrespect him this way. Miguel fired off another message: *"You know when you arrange to meet someone it's rude to cancel."*

For the next hour, there was nothing but silence. Miguel decided to send Mary another message to try and fix the situation: *"Hey, I just wanted to say I'm sorry I was angry before. I'm not angry at you. I was just disappointed because I really wanted to see you. Let me know when you're free and we can catch up."*

Miguel never heard back from Mary. His initial frustration and high level of emotional investment had turned Mary off and killed what little desire she had for him.

* * *

Almost a year ago to the day, Mary had been shopping at a new department store downtown when Jeff introduced himself. Jeff had asked for her number, and over the course of the following week, they both agreed to meet up on Saturday afternoon.

Jeff waited until Saturday morning before sending Mary a message: *"Hey, can meet at 7 pm?"*

About twenty minutes later, Mary responded with a similar message to the one she would later send Miguel: *"Hey, I'm really sorry but I can't make it this weekend. I'm really busy, maybe next week."*

Jeff didn't even bother to respond. As Mary waited for a response, she began to feel more and more anxious.

By late Saturday afternoon, Mary got the sense that

Jeff wasn't going to get back to her. She bit her lip. Maybe if I don't see him tonight I'll never see him again, she thought as she reached into her bag and pulled out her phone.

Jeff's phoned buzzed. He looked down and saw a message from Mary: *"Hey, looks like I can make it after all. Still on for 7?"*

⚔

The first time a woman flakes, a simple message saying: *"No problem, let me know when you're free"* should suffice. For added punch, you can also reference something you both previously talked about or a shared topic of interest. For example, if a woman told you she was obsessed with yoga, you could respond with a message that references your past conversation about yoga. When you reference a topic or shared interest, you bring the woman back to the moment when she first met you. The woman remembers why she liked you and why she gave you her number in the first place.

If a woman flakes more than twice, you must walk away from her and never contact her again unless she reaches out first. This also lets the woman know that you aren't going to chase her because you don't care if you see her or not. Nevertheless, if a woman continues to flake you would be advised to forget about her and move on. The reason why she flaked isn't so important, what is important is that the woman has shown through her actions that, for whatever reason, she's unwilling to meet you. A woman should always be judged by her actions, not her words.

Going no contact often fixes flaky behavior as it lets a woman know that you're not desperate and you have options with women. Furthermore, if a woman's testing you, going no contact will guarantee you pass her test with flying colors. On the other hand, if a woman's only looking for validation, going no contact lets her know that you aren't going to be there to feed her ego and give her the same validation that she gets from every other guy.

GOING NO CONTACT

The silence is deafening.

— Unknown

If a woman's interest level is currently low and you sense her pulling away from you, going no contact is one of the most effective ways to restore interest. If you're always the first to initiate contact and reach out in relationships, there's a good chance you're killing attraction. You're neither a mystery nor a challenge. Indeed, it's only when a woman feels a degree of uncertainty and anxiety that she starts to focus on a man and think more about him.

Research conducted at the University of Virginia came to the conclusion that men are rated as much more attractive and desirable when there's a degree of uncertainty and anxiety in the relationship.[74] And while you might hold the position that it's mean or rude to go no contact on a woman—that somehow you might hurt her feelings—you must focus on what *works* as opposed to what's *nice* if you want to build attraction. Going no contact is one of the best ways to get a woman focused on you and restore fading interest.

Nevertheless, when you go no contact on a woman, you must expect a degree of resistance. She might try to make you feel guilty for pulling away. She might berate you for ignoring her messages and threaten to cut you off. She might even play the innocent victim. In all these situations, you must never apologize for your behavior, for doing so would only ruin the seduction. A simple shrug of the shoulders accompanied by an "I've been busy" attitude is all that's required to diffuse the situation. And although this might sound Machiavellian, such is the nature of human attraction. Women who cry foul and deride men for "playing games" are simply infuriated that men now have the ability to neutralize a woman's long-held psychological advantage.

You must ensure, however, that you don't go no contact in a passive-aggressive way. Going no contact means a woman must reach out to you first. It might take an hour, it might take a day, it might take a week, it might even take a month. Regardless how long it takes, you must wait for a woman to get in touch with you first before you send her any more messages. When a woman reaches out to you, she's letting you know that she misses you and she's thinking about you. You must use this opportunity to establish rapport and ask her out on a date. It's that simple. Remember, seduction should be easy and never too complicated. The moment you feel a woman pull away from you, simply mirror her behavior and allow her space by going no contact. If you have the strength and confidence to give a woman space, she'll come back to you every time.

STOP APOLOGIZING

A man is sorry to be honest for nothing.

— Ovid

Research into conflict resolution has found that apologies are often accompanied by a loss of face and a loss of respect and status. A study published in the *European Journal of Social Psychology* found that people who refuse to apologize often feel better about themselves and have a greater sense of control over situations.[75] This doesn't mean you should never apologize under any circumstance. If you've lied, cheated, or caused some other misdemeanor, it's okay to apologize once and let a woman know it wasn't your intention to hurt her. In situations like this, it's always better to say, "I apologize" as opposed to "I'm sorry" as saying sorry makes a person appear more vulnerable compared to the less contrite "I apologize." If a woman still doesn't accept your apology, and she continues to call you a "cheater," "untrustworthy," or a "liar" you must respond with indifference to prevent the situation from spiraling out of control.

In the realm of attraction, it's not a crime to cheat, lie, and break promises. It is, however, a crime to repeatedly apologize for mistakes that were—rightly or wrongly—made in the past. If you assume the mantle of the eternal apologist, you'll not only pay the price for your transgressions now, but you'll continue to pay the price for your transgressions well into the future. Research into conflict resolution found that people who apologize on a frequent basis are more likely to be punished because their apology is seen as an admission of guilt.[75]

One key factor that must be considered is the way women perceive men who apologize. The apologetic man is considered weak and untrustworthy. If you cheat, or lie, or commit some other delightful sin, you must own your behavior and act without apology. A woman will only punish you for as long as you allow yourself to be punished. The moment you adopt a "get over it and move on" attitude is the moment a woman loses her ability to punish you. She can no longer make you feel guilt or remorse. Her attack is rendered useless, a senseless act of futility that serves no purpose other than to strengthen your position and make her look foolish.

PART THREE

BUILD ATTRACTION

*Pursuit and seduction are the essence of
sexuality. It's part of the sizzle.*

— Camille Paglia

Boy meets girl. Boy courts girl. Boy and girl have sex.
This is the natural flow of the seduction process. At
any point in time, however, the seduction process can
be derailed, leading to the death of attraction and a
failure to copulate. If you take a moment to analyze
the seduction process in more detail, you'll discover
that the seduction process can be broken down into
two distinct stages: "first contact" and "the chase."

STAGE ONE: FIRST CONTACT

At a basic level, the natural seduction process is easy
to follow. All you have to do is meet a woman you
like, create attraction, then consummate the
relationship. It should be noted, however, that just
because you get a woman's number doesn't mean the
seduction will move forward without resistance;
instead, getting a woman's number simply allows you
to test the waters and see if she's open to being

seduced. The moment you establish contact with a woman is the moment you get a sense of where she's at and whether or not she finds you attractive. This is the point where you begin to feel a woman out and get a sense of her baseline rate of attraction. Keep in mind, not all women are going to feel the same way about you right from the start. As the saying goes: 30 percent will love you, 30 percent will like you, and 30 percent will be indifferent towards you.

STAGE TWO: THE CHASE

The second stage of the seduction process, which is all about creating attraction and elevating a woman's desire for you is the most crucial stage of the seduction process. This is the stage where most relationship problems arise and the point where most women pull away and go cold for no apparent reason. It's at this stage that attraction either thrives or dies. At this stage of the seduction process, you're attempting to seduce a woman, and she's deciding whether or not she's going to allow you to seduce her or not.

At the beginning of the relationship, the man usually pursues the woman. This is the natural way of things, and you must ensure you strike a delicate balance between pursuing too much and showing just the right amount of desire. You must be proactive and bold without appearing desperate. By this stage, if everything goes well the woman will start to warm up to you. Once you sense a change in her behavior and notice that the woman is becoming more responsive, you must back off and allow her to chase to you.

One of the biggest mistakes men make is to come

across as overly desperate in the early stages of the relationship, bombarding women with messages and phone calls as they try to chase the woman into commitment. Men who do this are fearful that if they wait too long, another man will swoop in and steal the woman away. These men often roll out the same tired, old phrases: "I've never felt this way about a girl before" and "I think I might be falling in love with you" followed by the inevitable "When are you free? Anytime is good for me." And while these emotional expressions might appear romantic on the surface, all they really do is communicate weakness and desperation. Building attraction is like building a house. If you want to build a house that's strong and stable, you must first lay the right foundations.

NEVER RUSH THE SEDUCTION PROCESS

Fools rush in where angels fear to tread.

— Alexander Pope

In the grand cathedral that is your relationship, you must consider how you construct your temple. Do you build your temple like a cage to trap a woman? Or do you let a woman construct her temple around you, knowing full well that no matter what she does, she can never own you for you're a man who's born free and will remain free until the day you die.

CASE STUDY #15: 'TIL LOVE DO US PART

Vanessa and Eric couldn't keep their hands off each other. The sex was fantastic and their relationship was full of excitement and passion. Vanessa could tell Eric was infatuated with her, and it was intoxicating to be around someone who found her so attractive. Nevertheless, Vanessa was surprised to hear Eric confess his love only a month into the relationship. Eric said he couldn't imagine living without her and he was ready to settle down with someone he truly loved. This was music to Vanessa's ears. Her ex-boyfriends had all been horrible, selfish men who only cared about themselves. Now, finally, here was a man who genuinely loved her and wanted to be in a committed relationship.

You can imagine Eric's surprise when a couple of weeks later Vanessa told him she needed space. Confused, Eric fell into a blind panic. Why was Vanessa pulling away from him now when all he'd done was show her love and devotion? Something wasn't right. When Eric confronted Vanessa, she apologized for pulling away. She told Eric it wasn't his fault. "You're a great guy and you deserve to be with a woman who loves you and respects you."

Overcome with emotion, Eric began to tear up. "But we're so great together," Eric said.

"We were, we are... I don't know what happened... I just need some time to myself," Vanessa replied. And she wasn't lying. Vanessa genuinely didn't know why she had lost attraction for Eric. She couldn't understand her feelings and was at an utter loss to explain what was going on. All she knew was that she needed space and needed time to herself.

In reality, Eric had slowly killed attraction by continually expressing his desire to be in a committed relationship. This told Vanessa that Eric wanted the relationship more than she did. After a couple of weeks, Vanessa started to realize that Eric was fundamentally weak and relationship focused. He was the polar opposite of what a confident man should be. Vanessa knew strength when she saw it and Eric was anything but strong.

⋏

At the start of a blossoming romance, it's easy to get swept away by your emotions only to realize later that the relationship is moving too fast. It must be the man's fault, the woman reasons, for only a weak man would allow himself to be ensnared so quickly with such little resistance. When a woman comes to realize that the man is the one who's always expressing his love and devotion, alarm bells start ringing. You're the one who's always reaching out to her, seeking warmth and comfort in her embrace. Once, twice, and it barely registers. But slowly, over time the message couldn't be clearer: you care more; you need her more; and as a result, she comes to the sudden realization that you want the relationship more than she does. This is the primary reason why you must never rush the seduction process.

NEVER INVEST TOO MUCH TOO SOON

Never commit all to one boat.

— Latin Proverb

In the early stages of a relationship, dating should be simple and relaxed. A date shouldn't be expensive and it shouldn't require excessive planning. You don't need to think about taking a woman to an overpriced restaurant, in the same way you don't need to plan an expensive trip to Paris to win her over. Spend too much money too soon and a woman will wonder why you're trying so hard to impress her. The unattractive man feels the need to impress; the attractive man knows his presence is enough.

CASE STUDY #16: THE PERILS OF OVER INVESTING

Ted was at a rock concert when he saw Lauren for the first time. She was standing with her eyes closed, swaying to the music in a tight-fitting black dress. As soon as the concert finished, Ted rushed over to Lauren and introduced himself. After some light chitchat, they exchanged numbers and went their separate ways.

For the next couple of weeks, Ted texted Lauren on

a daily basis. But it didn't matter how much he texted her, he found it impossible to get her out on a date. Frustrated by Lauren's resistance, Ted decided to go all out and invite Lauren to an expensive restaurant for dinner. The restaurant had amazing city views, and the cost of dinner was $200 per head. Lauren was delighted to get Ted's invitation. Without skipping a beat, she got on the phone and told her best friend Lisa where she was going.

"Oh, I'm so jealous. Who are you going with?" Lisa asked.

"Just some guy, but he's paying for it, so it's all good," Lauren replied.

Poor Ted. He had no idea that once their night of fine dining was over, he would never see or hear from Lauren again. Lauren knew all too well that Ted was only buying her dinner because he wanted to get into her pants, but Lauren was too smart to fall for that old trick. In her mind, the plan was simple—get the free dinner, take some pictures, then go home. After all, a man like Ted was lucky to be graced by her presence. She was a beautiful, elegant woman, and he thought he could buy her love? What a loser.

᠕

It's logical to assume that women will appreciate you going the extra mile to make them feel special; and on the surface, it's true, a woman might appreciate your initial effort to make her feel comfortable. Scratch a little deeper, however, and you'll soon discover that women are wary of men who try too hard to impress them. Are you trying to buy her approval? Are you trying to buy her love? In an effort to impress, a man might talk endlessly about his achievements and why he's such a great catch, all the while forgetting—*less is more.*

Why are movies and TV shows so popular? Why are people willing to sit in suspense hour after hour to find out how their favorite TV show will end? People are curious by nature, and no one is more curious than a woman. Women crave suspense and "not knowing" drives them wild. The man who gives away too much too soon leaves no room to the imagination and offers little in the way of mystery or suspense. He has given away the end of the movie before its even begun.

The following scenario is played out time and time again: man meets woman. Man begins to imagine all the great sex they'll have together; he imagines all the adventures and trips they'll go on together; he even imagines getting married and having children. One trait that is uniquely human is our ability to perform wonderful feats of mental time travel, known as *chronesthesia*. Chronesthesia is a term that refers to the human ability to travel into the future and predict what might happen if we perform certain actions. For example, you know that if you invest five dollars today, it might be worth twenty dollars in the future. And you know that if you ask a girl out, she might say yes or she might say no. Every time you predict a possible future event, you're performing an act of chronesthesia. One of the great disadvantages of chronesthesia, however, is that people often imagine positive future scenarios that lead them to invest too much of their emotions and time into someone in an irrational way.

Research into mental time travel has discovered a strong connection between mental disorders and chronesthesia.[76] These mental disorders usually occur when a person imagines too many negative future events that ultimately lead to high levels of anxiety, depression, and neuroticism. The same damage occurs when a person projects too many positive future events onto one person only to discover later that these positive future events are unlikely to come true.

CASE STUDY #17: FAST LOVE IS CHEAP LOVE

Ray had just finished playing tennis when he met Lorraine, relaxing with a gin and tonic in the clubhouse overlooking the courts. From day one, Ray and Lorraine were drawn to each other. Ray couldn't stop thinking about Lorraine. She was sexy, funny, athletic, and sassy—she was everything he loved in a woman. When Ray thought about Lorraine, he could already see their future mapped out together: the big house, lots of kids, and fun-filled family vacations in the Caribbean.

Last week, Ray and Lorraine had spent the entire weekend hanging out, having sex, and watching their favorite TV show. It had been the perfect weekend, and Ray couldn't wait to do it all over again the following week.

For her part, Lorraine enjoyed Ray's company; however, she couldn't shake the nagging feeling that Ray was way more into her than she was into him. This became all the more apparent when Ray told her how much he had enjoyed their weekend together, and that he couldn't wait to see her again soon.

On Monday afternoon, Ray reached out with another love-infused message: *"Hey, sweetheart. How's your day?"*

Lorraine cringed when she read the message. This was all happening too fast, she had only just met the guy and he was already telling her how much he missed her and was even calling her "sweetheart." Lorraine grabbed her phone and told Ray she was busy for the next couple of weeks. Little did Ray know he would spend the next two years trying, without success, to get Lorraine to see him again.

⋏

How much are you willing to invest in a woman? Are you willing to invest 100 percent of your emotions, 50 percent, 20 percent, or less than 10 percent? When you invest 100 percent of your emotions into a woman, you inadvertently lay the foundation for your own demise. The over-invested man is only too willing to open his heart and give his love away. He lets a woman know he's there for her and is responsive to her needs and desires. On the other hand, the man who chooses to hold back is more likely to win a woman over and inspire feelings of attraction. The man who holds back doesn't invest too much too soon. Instead, he sets himself up as a challenge and becomes a man whose love is hard to acquire.

The wise man chooses to hold back his emotions in case the relationship goes south, and he discovers that he's dating a woman who's either unstable, incompatible, or unworthy of long-term emotional investment. By holding back on your emotions, you automatically become more attractive because you're neither focused on the relationship or its outcome. You keep your options open and you're reluctant to give away your freedom and independence because you value those things above all else. As research published in the *European Journal of Personality* points out, if a woman has to fight for a man's love and attention, she'll think more highly of him, value him more, and think about him more frequently.[91] How do you make yourself more valuable? First, you must make your love a scarce resource—something that's hard to acquire. This all starts by refusing to invest too much of your emotions into a woman too soon. Emotional investment in a relationship should be a slow, gradual process. The attractive man holds back and never gives his love away too easily.

MAINTAIN MYSTERY

EASE, JOY, ITS AVAILABILITY VERSUS MYSTERY

*It is the dim haze of mystery that
adds enchantment to pursuit.*

— Antoine Rivarol

When you first meet a woman, it's tempting to open up and tell her as much about yourself as possible. And while you might initially be rewarded for your candid disclosure, you'll inevitably be punished later on for having given away too much information too soon. Instead, you must use the elements of mystery and challenge to your advantage. If you spend countless hours sending messages back and forth, texting and calling a woman, talking about your life, your dreams, and what you had for dinner, you inadvertently kill attraction by revealing too much information. When you over-communicate, you not only risk revealing too much about yourself, you risk killing attraction by being too available and responsive. Regardless of whether or not you want to see a woman, it's always advisable to keep the calls and messages to a minimum. That doesn't mean you must act cold and distant, but it does mean you should be aware of the dangers of over communication.

In the early stages of a relationship, it's important not to move too fast. There's a tendency to worry that if you don't get a woman out on a date as fast as possible, she'll forget about you and move on. You must have enough confidence in yourself to know that a woman won't be able to forget about you that easily.

CASE STUDY #18: AVAILABILITY VERSUS MYSTERY

Ingrid was a successful, attractive businesswoman in her mid-thirties. But because Ingrid worked so much, she rarely, if ever, had a chance to socialize. That was why she was so surprised when last week, at a trade show, she met two attractive guys, Ken and Phil, within the space of an afternoon. Ingrid felt a rush of excitement as she left the convention center. She had forgotten what it felt like to feel wanted and desired— let alone wanted and desired by two men at the same time.

On Sunday morning, Ingrid checked her phone and saw two messages: one from Ken and one from Phil. Both men asked how she was doing, and Ingrid responded by telling them that she was heading out of town on a business trip for a couple of days.

On Monday evening, Ingrid received another message from Ken. Ingrid and Ken chatted for twenty minutes before Ken said good night.

On Tuesday morning, Ingrid received a message from Ken and a message from Phil. Ken sent his customary *"Good morning"* message, while Phil simply asked Ingrid how long she would be going away for. Ingrid responded to both men before heading off to work.

That afternoon, Ingrid received another message from Ken. They chitchatted for ten minutes before Ingrid told Ken she had to get back to work.

Later that day, Ingrid received another message

from Ken while she was in the shower. Ken told her how much he was looking forward to seeing her when she was back in town.

On Wednesday morning, Ingrid received a good morning message from Ken and nothing from Phil. Ingrid had a quick conversation with Ken as she lay in bed, wondering briefly, for a moment, if she would ever hear from Phil again. Ken was a nice guy. He liked to share his day with her and seemed to be genuinely interested in what was going on in her life. Phil, on the other hand, gave the impression that he wasn't all that interested in getting to know her. That's a shame, Ingrid thought, he was cute.

On Thursday morning, Ingrid woke up to the usual good morning message from Ken. They chatted for about twenty minutes before Ken invited her out for dinner on Saturday night. With no other plans, Ingrid said yes. As for Phil, Ingrid hadn't heard a peep from him since Tuesday. Ingrid wondered if she would ever hear from him again, maybe he was just being polite when he asked for her number.

On Friday, Ingrid received a couple more messages from Ken, no surprise there. Ken told her again how much he was looking forward to seeing her on the weekend. Then, on Friday afternoon, Ingrid received an unexpected message from Phil, asking if she'd like to meet up for drinks on Saturday evening.

Ingrid didn't know what to say. Ken had already booked dinner for the two of them. She couldn't just cancel on him now, could she? Ingrid couldn't put her finger on it, but she had the feeling that if she didn't see Phil on Saturday she might never see him again. She also knew that if she canceled on Ken they could easily reschedule to meet up another time later in the week. After thinking it over for a couple of minutes, Ingrid decided to cancel her date with Ken and meet Phil instead. And although both men were attractive, Ingrid's intuition told her that out of the two men, Phil was the more confident, high-value option. Her intuition, in this case, turned out to be correct.

⋏

The compulsive need to reveal too much information about yourself and your feelings must be repressed. How can a woman find you mysterious when she knows exactly what you're thinking on a day-to-day basis? Wearing your heart on your sleeve and expressing your innermost feelings spoils intrigue and crushes desire. Less is more. Less initial effort, less initial investment, and less initial expenditure shows a woman that you're not actively seeking a relationship. This helps foster a more relaxed environment, an environment that's conducive to seduction. Instead of being relationship focused, you must keep the conversation light and playful. Tease a woman, have fun, and never take her or yourself too seriously. The more time you spend talking to a woman, the more she gets to know you and the more comfortable and secure she'll feel in your presence. Your mission, however, is to remain slightly unknowable and mysterious in the early stages of a relationship.

You should never allow a woman full access to your mind. The misguided belief that you should share your innermost thoughts and feelings is an illusion propagated by a *tell her all your feelings and she'll love you for it* culture. Many men have traveled this road before with disastrous consequences. All too often I see men open their hearts only to see women respond with a loss of attraction. How could this happen? What happened to the wonderful connection they both shared? The next time you think about opening up to a woman ask yourself this: what are you trying to achieve? Sympathy? Understanding? Reassurance? A sense of closeness? If that's the case, you'd be better off seeking solace in friends and family, for self-disclosure and attraction rarely go hand-in-hand. Men of mystery are attractive because they understand that less is more and women need to be challenged.

EXPLOIT HER WEAKNESS FOR WORDS

*Words are of course the most powerful
drug used by mankind.*

— Rudyard Kipling

A man and woman sit next to each other in a quiet bar. "Who's the most important person in your life right now?" the man says.

The woman thinks for a moment. "Person? Well, my parents, my family, my friends, umm, the people close to me," she says with a smile. "How about you, who's the most important person in your life?"

The man looks deep into the woman's eyes and says only one word, "You." The woman flinches. "I might not see you again, but right now you're here with me and I'm here with you. You're the most important person in my life right now." And with that the woman falls completely under the man's spell. Such is the power of words.

It's not uncommon for a man to become weak and vulnerable in the presence of a beautiful woman. Indeed, a woman's beauty is her main asset. And just as men have a weakness for beauty, women have a weakness for words. Women, being primarily auditory creatures, are influenced more than anything by what they hear as opposed to what they see. This is in sharp contrast to men who tend to focus on what they see as opposed to what they hear.

It doesn't matter how far along in the seduction process you are, whether you're dating a girl for the first time or you've been dating her for years, the way you communicate with women should always be light and relaxed. Serious talk is anti-seductive and the death knell of attraction. Talking about serious subjects (like business, the economy, and politics) does nothing to stimulate attraction or inspire interest in women. If you feel the need to brag about your achievements or about how great and successful you are, a woman will sense your need to impress. The confident man doesn't feel the need to brag or talk about his achievements; instead, he lets his behavior and actions speak for themselves.

When talking to women, it's important not to overthink what you say. All you have to do is remain relaxed and open to the fluidity that is human conversation. A study published in the *Journal of Personal Relationships* made headlines when it claimed that men who have strong storytelling abilities are perceived to be more powerful, high status, and attractive to women. This is particularly true when a woman is considering a man for a long-term relationship.[77] The study suggests that men who are good storytellers can convey social intelligence in a way that demonstrates high-status and value. However, strong storytelling ability was found to have no effect on women who were looking for short-term relationships. Still, another study published in the *Journal of Personality and Social Psychology* found that men who were more prosocial and outgoing were rated more sexually attractive compared to less prosocial men.[78] The key to building attraction with words, according to a study published in the *Journal of Personal Relationships*, is to tell "fluid" stories packed with "lively vocabulary" as opposed to telling stories that are boring, uninteresting, and highly detailed. In other words, keep it interesting and never labor your point.

Men have a natural tendency to want to communicate logically. Women, however, prefer to engage their emotions when they communicate. The ability to talk about a variety of topics and explore deeper feelings is a significant component of female communication. The man who engages his emotions and feelings and "lets go" in conversation has a distinct and significant advantage when it comes to building attraction. In fact, being able to talk naturally about a wide variety of topics is a key marker of intelligence. You don't have to talk about intelligent topics or lace your conversations with facts, but you do need to engage a woman's emotions and speak about various topics in a fluid and engaging way.

Studies show that engaging conversationalists are seen as more attractive compared to dull, inhibited conversationalists who are viewed as not only less attractive but less likable as well.[79] There's a reason why good communicators find it easier to seduce women. They know how to talk and what they say is never boring. The charming conversationalist has no qualms talking about things that are controversial or politically incorrect. Men with lively conversation styles usually live lives filled with adventure and risk. Attractive men go out into the world and collect wonderful stories and memories along the way. Their ability to regale a woman with their adventures and use colorful language is simply a by-product of living a full and interesting life, something that every man should aspire to.

Women fall for charming men, not because these men are necessarily handsome or particularly successful, but because these men know how to use words to their advantage. Men who can tell stories and amusing anecdotes hold a significant advantage in the realm of seduction. Researchers at the University of North Carolina at Chapel Hill and SUNY Buffalo confirmed this theory with a series of long-running experiments.[80] The researchers discovered that women were more attracted to men who had good storytelling abilities compared to men who rarely told stories. Men who were able to recount memorable experiences, anecdotes or stories were perceived as more socially intelligent and desirable. Furthermore, the researchers found that a man's ability to use words skillfully to entertain and charm indicates that the man was more likely to be popular and have good leadership potential. It should be noted that using words to charm doesn't require great skill or unassailable talent. To charm a woman, all you have to do is engage her on a wide variety of topics to elicit an emotional response. To strengthen the connection between yourself and a woman, you mustn't be afraid to show your vulnerable side, if only for a moment.

No one likes to be around people who appear too perfect and in control all the time. If you appear too perfect, you run the risk of alienating women as well as the people around you. Instead, you must show occasional moments of vulnerability by opening up and revealing small, intimate details about your life. Moments of candid self-disclosure can also help to lower a woman's defenses. Still, you must remember not to reveal too much too soon. When you disclose personal information, you must only let a woman catch a brief glimpse of your soul before closing yourself back up again. Indeed, it's been found that brief moments of candid self-disclosure allow a woman to feel greater levels of trust and comfort.[81] If you aim to create a close connection with a woman, there's no better way to achieve this than to ask the occasional penetrating question peppered with selective self-disclosure.

All humans have insecurities and frustrations that we must deal with on a daily basis. Such is the nature of life. Your ability to show moments of empathy tinged with vulnerability is an endearing quality in a harsh and unforgiving world. If you truly want to connect with women, first you must learn to relate to them through shared experience and emotion. This is one reason why books and movies are such popular forms of entertainment. Humans have an insatiable appetite for stories. Stories are the means by which we relate to the world and the people around us. When communicating, you must give a woman the chance to open up and talk about herself. Talking about herself is, after all, a woman's favorite topic. And the more a woman talks about herself, the more you cultivate an aura of mystery. You listen to her with intent and get to know her innermost thoughts. This, in turn, allows you to connect with her on a deeper level. Yet still she knows almost nothing about you.

Who are you? What are you thinking? What do you want? Women are curious by nature and the more information you withhold, the more curious she becomes. And once you add flattery into the equation, the effect becomes almost intoxicating.

Imagine for a moment that you've just been introduced to your friend's colleague Jim. A couple of days later, your friend tells you that Jim thought you were "interesting" and "funny." As a result, you can't help but like Jim even though you've only just met him. This is the power of the *likability effect*. A group of researchers, investigating the likability effect, conducted a study where two strangers were asked to have a conversation with each other.[82] One person was a participant while the other person was an actor working for the researchers. After the participant and actor had finished their conversation, they were asked to make a brief statement, rating the other person. After making their statements, each person was then allowed to read what the other person wrote about them. The results of the study showed that when the actor rated the other person highly and said positive things about them, the other person was more likely to feel the same way and "like" the actor in response.

Women always find it hard to resist flattery and attention. The key is to find something about the woman that you like and use it to your advantage. Is it her hair, her smell, her clothes, or her general sense of style and elegance that you find appealing? Whatever it is, don't be afraid to vocalize it and let the woman know what it is you like about her. When you tell a woman, in no uncertain terms, that you're attracted to her and find her desirable, you exploit the power of the likability effect.

Flattery will get you everywhere, and a well-placed compliment can easily disarm even the most challenging woman. The key, as always, is to keep a woman off-balance and remain unpredictable. You should never shower a woman with too many compliments; instead, you must hold back just enough to allow an element of doubt to creep into the woman's mind and make her wonder whether or not you really do like her. Uncertainty, after all, is more attractive than certainty.

THE MAGIC OF TOUCH

Too often we underestimate the power of touch.

— Leo Buscaglia

The moment we're born, we crave touch. Touch has an almost intoxicating effect on the human body. A woman runs her hand through your hair, then softly touches your chest before kissing you. A bolt of electricity shoots down your spine, and you feel wonderful as a wave of oxytocin courses through your body. Touch expresses your intentions and desires in a way that words cannot. There's no need to tell a woman that you want to become intimate with her. If you touch her the right way, she'll know what you're thinking.

Touch wields enormous power and influence. If you ask someone to do something for you and touch the person at the same time, that person is much more likely to comply with your request. Studies into influence and touch have confirmed this finding. One study found that a man who asked a woman for her phone number and followed his request with a light touch on the arm was much more likely to gain compliance from the woman and get her phone number. Another interesting study examined what would happen when a man asked a woman to dance in a nightclub. The study found that the man's request was more likely to be accepted if the man touched the woman on the arm for one or two seconds before asking her to dance.[83] The implications of this study are far-reaching and powerful. What is it about touch that increases a woman's compliance? In both of these experiments, after the woman complied with the man's request to either "get her phone number" or "dance," the woman was asked to fill out a survey to explain her feelings during the experiment. The women explained that they felt as though the man who touched her was more confident, and as a result, they felt more inclined to comply with his request.

Further research into this phenomenon has found that touch creates feelings of attraction in both men and women.[84] Not only does touch build attraction, touch also makes a woman's heart beat faster and leads to increased feelings of desire, especially when accompanied by eye contact.[85] Only one question remains: are you bold enough and confident enough to touch a woman the right way?

Touch a woman the right way and you pour rocket fuel on the flames of attraction; touch her the wrong way, however, and there's a good chance you'll turn her off and she'll lose attraction for you. In the same way, if you touch a woman too frequently and too soon, you run the risk of smothering the woman and making her feel uncomfortable. The same applies if your touch is clumsy.

A lack of finesse will make you look uncertain and unsure of yourself. When you touch a woman, you must touch her with confidence and boldness. You must reach out to her and commit to the touch. Allow her to feel you, if only for a brief second, before pulling away.

With this in mind, when you first start dating a woman, there's no need to be distant. Hug a woman. Embrace her. Allow her to feel you because your touch sets the tone for the rest of the encounter. If you sit beside a woman while watching a movie, lean in and touch her on the arm whenever you say something. The same applies if you go for dinner or go out for drinks. Sit beside your date and position yourself so your hand can brush up against her hand. Don't attempt to kiss a woman in public or smother her with excessive touching. Doing so will only ruin the seduction and build resistance.

Your goal, as with all seductions, is to be patient and build the fire of attraction into a raging inferno. When you touch a woman's hand, forearm, shoulder or back, you put her at ease and give her a sense of comfort. Even if she pulls away from you or tells you that you're moving too fast, the fact that she's still with you shows that she wants you to keep trying. There will be occasions when you touch a woman and she doesn't respond. She might even cross her arms and physically pull away from you. Expect a degree of resistance, especially early on, but don't let it stop you from pushing for intimacy.

A woman will never punish you for trying to have sex with her. She'll only punish you if you apologize for your actions. Going back on your actions is a form of weakness and a huge turn-off to women. As a man, you must be bold and push for physical intimacy, even if you encounter resistance—resistance, after all, is simply a woman's way of testing you.

CASE STUDY #19: NEVER SEEK A WOMAN'S TOUCH

Alex and Grace had been together for almost six blissful months when one day, while walking down the street, Grace unexpectedly pulled away from Alex and let go of his hand. Alex immediately felt unsettled and anxious. Why's she pulling away from me? he thought. Have I done something wrong?

"Are you okay?" Alex asked.

"I'm fine," Grace replied as she continued to walk beside him with her arms folded across her chest.

* * *

Later that week, Alex and Grace were sitting on the couch, watching TV, with their arms wrapped around each other when Grace suddenly pulled away from Alex and moved over to the far side of the couch.

"You okay?" Alex asked, an edge of anxiety creeping into his voice.

"Uh-huh," Grace muttered, staring at the TV.

"You're not getting away that easy," Alex said as he shuffled over towards Grace and wrapped his arms around her, holding her firmly from behind. Grace immediately stiffened and pulled away. "What is it, what's wrong?"

"Why do you have to touch me all the time?" Grace said.

"I'm not."

"What's wrong with you?" Grace snapped. "Why are you so clingy?"

"I'm not clingy, why do you keep pulling away from me?" Alex said as a well of emotion built up inside him.

"Wait, oh my God. Are you crying?"

"No."

"You are." Alex turned his head, but it was too late. Grace had already seen the tears. "Stop being so sensitive," Grace said.

"I'm not," Alex shot back.

Grace got up from the couch and grabbed her keys off the table. "God, you're acting like a woman. It's so unattractive."

⅄

There will be moments in a relationship when a woman purposefully holds back, making it a point to introduce distance between the two of you. She neither reaches for you nor welcomes your touch. This has the effect of bringing a certain level of tension and anxiety into the relationship. Why doesn't she want to touch me, is she pulling away from me? the man thinks. And with that, the man reaches out to try and close the distance, wondering all along why the woman doesn't want to touch him and why she's being so cold?

There are many reasons why a woman might act this way. She might be testing you to see how you'll react. Will you feel uncomfortable and insecure or will you remain strong and unaffected by her withdrawal? At other times, she might simply be asking for space. In both situations, you must let a woman pull away from you without feeling the need to reach out and seek her touch.

At this stage, it's important to distinguish between two different types of touch. Brief touching on the arm, shoulder, and back is closely aligned with flirtatious, non-needy playful behavior. On the other hand, holding a woman's hand, hugging, and embracing is more closely aligned with needy, clingy behavior. Initiate the second type of touch too frequently and the woman will come to think that you need her more than she needs you. Once this realization sets in, the woman's attraction for you will inevitably fade.

Research published in the *Personality and Social Psychology Bulletin* observed that women rated men who displayed traits of neediness and insecurity as extremely unattractive.[86] How can a woman trust you when all she has to do is withdraw her touch to upset you? The secure and confident man never seeks a woman's touch for comfort or validation.

CASE STUDY #20: TOO TIMID TO TOUCH

Sarah, an elegant woman in her mid-thirties, was talking to two men, Richard and Joe, at the same time. It was Richard, however, who made the first move, inviting Sarah out for coffee over the weekend. When Sarah and Richard started talking to each other they were both struck by how much they had in common. For one, they had both graduated from the same college. They also loved the same kind of movies and the same kind of music. Sarah had a great feeling about Richard. He was the perfect gentleman. He didn't try to touch her or come on too strong. Instead, he appeared to be genuinely interested in who she was and what she had to say.

A couple of days later, Sarah accepted Joe's

invitation to go out for dinner. The moment Joe picked her up, Sarah was taken aback by his brash behavior. Right from the start, Joe came across as selfish and self-centered. Sarah didn't care for his manners either. When they got to the restaurant, she noted with dismay that Joe never once said "please" or "thank you" to the wait staff. To make matters worse, Joe didn't even seem that interested in anything she had to say, and he even openly disagreed with her on several occasions. Sarah didn't like his attitude. But despite the many red flags, there was something about Joe that intrigued her. Yes, he was rude and arrogant, that was true. But he was also interesting. He flirted like crazy and didn't hesitate when it came to touching her.

When she got home, Sarah felt confused. She had nothing in common with Joe, but she'd still enjoyed their time together. When Richard called to schedule another date, Sarah was surprised to discover that she no longer had any interest in seeing him. Richard seemed so flat and lifeless in comparison to Joe. Asshole or not, Joe was exciting and fun to be around. For better or worse, he was exactly the type of guy Sarah found attractive.

***

Why did Sarah choose Joe over Richard? The answer, again, comes down to attraction. Sarah felt a greater level of attraction for Joe compared to Richard. Joe's body language and actions were bolder and more confident. He wasn't afraid to call her out and disagree with her. And he wasn't afraid to signal his interest by touching her. This was in stark contrast to

Richard who came across as timid and shy in comparison.

⋏

When you're out on a date, talking is the easy part. Taking the interaction from friendly chitchat to playful touch, however, is what separates the attractive man from the unattractive man. Your ability to escalate the interaction and become physical with a woman is of paramount importance. A woman knows you're interested in her the moment you ask her out. Why not demonstrate your interest in a physical way? After all, she's not dating you because she wants to be your friend.

GET HER TO CHASE YOU

*If a woman doesn't chase a man
a little, she doesn't love him.*

— E. W. Howe

Women are taught from an early age that it's the man's job to do the chasing. This is only half-true. When a man seduces a woman, he chases her, makes his move, and pushes through the woman's initial resistance to become physically intimate with her. It's at this point that the woman transitions from being passive (allowing the man to chase her) to being proactive (where she actively chases the man).

A successful seduction requires you to let go and stop chasing. You must let a woman come to you and express her interest in you by allowing her to chase you. If you fail to allow this transition to take place, don't be surprised if the woman loses attraction for you and pulls away. The moment you focus on the relationship is the moment a woman starts to lose attraction. It's tempting to tell a woman how you feel about her as though this will somehow soften her emotions and make her easier to seduce. When a man is focused on the relationship, he derails the seduction process. The woman used to dream of the day when a man would come along and sweep her off her feet. But when that day finally arrives something inside the woman tells her that love shouldn't be this way, and she's right, it shouldn't.

One of the problems we face as men is a natural discomfort at the speed with which women respond to messages, want to see us, and are willing to progress the relationship. All this can leave a man feeling uncomfortable and uncertain about where he stands and where the relationship is headed. A woman knows when you're chasing her out of desire as opposed to chasing her out of insecurity. This insecurity often leads men to take action in an attempt to gain clarity and calm their nerves, but instead of feeling calm, the man inadvertently pushes the woman further away from him.

Given a choice between freedom and commitment, you must always choose freedom. An attractive man is a man with options. Why would you want to sacrifice your options for the sake of one woman? Instead, if a woman chases you, she can only draw one conclusion: you must be high-value otherwise she wouldn't be chasing you. Still, women continue to churn out the usual clichés: "If a man likes me, he should chase me" and "Women don't chase, that's a man's job." If you buy into this way of thinking, you become just another weak, beta male in hot pursuit. Your strength as a man lies in your ability to remain indifferent to a woman's behavior, whether she's chasing you or not.

Getting a woman to chase you is a subtle process. There are, however, certain techniques you can use to ensure a woman chases you and becomes more attracted to you. First, you must have the inner-strength to allow a woman to reach out to you. It's always a good idea to adhere to the 80/20 rule. The 80/20 rule is a powerful concept that governs many areas of life, not just relationships. For example, 80 percent of a company's profit often comes from 20 percent of its customers; 80 percent of the world's population lives in approximately 20 percent of the world's land mass; 80 percent of the world's wealth is owned by approximately 20 percent of the world's population. The 80/20 rule, when applied to male/female relationships, states that a man should reach out to a woman 20 percent of the time, and a woman should reach out to the man 80 percent of the time. Here, the 80/20 rule ensures the woman chases the man, and it also ensures there's enough space and distance between the woman and the man for attraction to flourish.

CASE STUDY #21: NEVER CHASE ATTRACTION

A week before Valentine's Day, Sam booked a trip for himself and his girlfriend to Grenada in the Caribbean. Sam was doing well financially and he didn't mind paying for the holiday. After all, he was a generous guy. When Sam got to Grenada with his girlfriend, Annie, the first thing they did was check into a beautiful five-star resort. Sam hoped the resort would be the perfect environment to help resolve their two biggest relationship problems: no intimacy and no sex. Sam had been dating Annie for about four months, and so far, Annie had refused to have sex with him. Annie said she didn't want to rush things because she was afraid to get hurt. Sam reasoned that Annie just needed a little more time to warm up.

A week later, Sam and Annie returned home, and instead of feeling relaxed, Sam was furious. During their time away, Annie had refused to have sex with him or even give him so much as a kiss. One night, at an all-time low, Sam had knelt beside the bed and begged Annie to have sex with him. From that point on their relationship had continued to deteriorate as Annie became increasingly rude and disrespectful. Despite all this, the moment Sam got home, he sent Annie a message, hoping to reconcile their differences and fix the relationship: *"Hey, hope you got home safe. Thanks for the trip. I miss you already X"* Sam waited for Annie to respond. An hour passed by, two hours passed by, three hours passed by... and still no response from Annie. This is bullshit; she's so disrespectful, Sam thought.

At first, Sam just wanted to get everything back to normal. However, when he realized that Annie wasn't going to play ball, he decided to change his approach and try to reason with her by sending her a heartfelt message: *"I know what we have is real. You have to understand that when we were on holiday together I didn't give you the opportunity to see the real me. Maybe I was holding back too. But I want you to know that I'm here for you now. Ready to love you and be with you completely. All I ask is that you give us another chance and you'll see how amazing our relationship can be."*

Annie responded a couple of hours later, and her response was anything but enthusiastic: *"Thanks for the holiday and the kind words."*

After a couple of weeks trying to be nice, Sam lost his cool and sent Annie a message laced with venom: *"Did I ever hurt you like your ex-boyfriends? Did I ever treat you with disrespect? Never. Did I go and have sex with other women then leave you like all your ex-boyfriends did? I was the* one who was always there for you and showed you what true love really is. What did I get in return? Nothing. Nothing but complete disrespect and BS. You didn't even want to kiss me on holiday. A holiday that I paid for. A holiday that cost me over $5,000! What I want to know is this, why did you have sex with your ex-boyfriends and not me?!?! They all treated you like shit and I treated you like a princess."

Annie cringed when she read the message. Thank God, I didn't have sex with him, that would have been a disaster. But hey, at least I got a free holiday out of it, Annie thought as she blocked Sam and deleted his number from her phone.

⅄

In the same way that you should never chase a woman over the phone, you must also refrain from chasing commitment. The moment you ask a woman that one fatal question: "Are we boyfriend and girlfriend?" is the moment she starts to question your masculinity. A woman will let you know when she wants to have a relationship with you, there's no need to chase commitment.

A series of studies published in the *European Journal of Personality* observed that less available men are perceived to be more attractive and desirable.[87] The researchers also discovered that people are willing to spend more money on less available people. In one of the studies, men were ranked as having either "low," "intermediate" or "high" availability. The female participants in the study were then asked whether or not they would be willing to spend their money to take one of the men out to a "fast food," "casual," or "fine dining" restaurant. The results of the study showed that the female participants were much more likely to take a man to a "fine dining" restaurant if the man had "low availability." This further explains why nice guys finish last. If you're too available, women can't help but see you as low value and less attractive. If a woman's chasing you, she's going to value you; and if she values you, she can't help but find you attractive.

THE POWER OF SEX

Sex is not only the basis of life,
it is the reason for life.

— Norman Lindsay

Men and women are biologically designed to come together to reproduce and ensure the survival of the species. In most cases, sex marks a definite turning point in the relationship. It's the moment when a woman physically submits to a man and allows him to become intimate with her. When a woman has sex, a series of powerful chemicals are released. This chemical release makes a woman feel closer to a man. During sex, the areas of the female brain that are affected by arousal are the amygdala, ventral tegmental area, nucleus accumbens, cerebellum, and the pituitary gland. One reason why sex has such a powerful effect on women is that it activates so many areas of the brain all at once. It's not so much that love is blind, but the chemicals within our bodies that make us blind.

A study published in the *Journal of Neuroscience* found that male and female brains light up like a person taking hcroin when experiencing orgasm.[88] A whole host of chemicals are responsible for this pleasure overload. First, a dopamine release lifts our mood and gives us feelings of pleasure. At the same time, prolactin relaxes us and makes us feel satisfied, while oxytocin makes us feel closer and more attached to the person we have sex with. It should be noted that oxytocin is released in much greater quantities in women than men. Finally, phenylethylamine, a stimulant that is also found in chocolate, improves our energy levels, and, at the same time, makes us feel happy. This is why sex is so addictive and powerful. The moment you have sex with a woman, there's a good chance she'll become addicted to you.

A man who understands the power of sex can make a woman fall in love with him simply by sleeping with her. There is, however, sex that increases attraction and sex that kills attraction. If you have sex in a weak and submissive way, you can still turn a woman off. So, what exactly constitutes weak, submissive sex?

CASE STUDY #22: UNCERTAINTY KILLS PASSION

Harry had been dating Chloe for almost two months, and this was the first time Chloe had been to his apartment. The moment Chloe arrived, Harry made her feel right at home. He took her coat then invited her in to watch *Some Like It Hot* (Chloe's favorite movie starring Marilyn Monroe). As Chloe relaxed, watching the movie, Harry went into the kitchen and brought out a big bowl of lasagna and a Greek salad. Chloe was impressed—this was homemade cooking at its finest.

Three hours later, Harry and Chloe were sitting on the couch together, sharing a bottle of wine. Time to make a move, Harry thought, but how?

An hour later, Harry still couldn't figure out how to make a move without being too obvious about it. It was then, after growing restless, that Chloe looked Harry straight in the eye and said, "Are you going to kiss me or not?"

"Sure, of course," Harry replied. "I'd love to."

Ten minutes later, Harry was lying in bed next to Chloe. "I want to kiss you again," Harry said as though waiting for Chloe to give him permission.

"No need to ask," Chloe whispered.

"I'm so excited, I can feel my heart racing." Harry stroked Chloe's face, then kissed her on the lips as he reached around to unfasten her bra. "I'm sorry, I can't undo it," he said.

Chloe reached behind her back and unfastened the clasp. She was now completely naked.

"You look amazing," Harry said.

"Thanks," Chloe whispered as Harry climbed on top of her and slowly inserted himself. Chloe flinched.

"Are you okay?" Harry asked.

"I'm not ready."

"Really?"

"Yeah."

"Is it okay?" Harry said as he pushed deeper inside her. Harry continued to thrust and wiggle on top of Chloe for a couple of minutes before she stopped him by placing her hand on his shoulder.

"What is it? Did I hurt you?"

"No, I'm sorry."

"What's wrong?"

"This isn't working," Chloe said as she pulled away from Harry and slid out from underneath him.

If you rush intimacy, you risk turning a woman off. In the same way, if you try too hard to please a woman, you're making the woman's pleasure more important than your own—this also turns women off. So how can you have sex with a woman and remain attractive? As always, it's important to seek intimacy without regret and without apology. You mustn't shy away from intimacy; instead, you must pursue it fearlessly. As with all things masculine, actions speak louder than words.

One issue that infects so many lesbian relationships is a phenomenon commonly referred to as *lesbian bed death*. Labeled "bed death" because lesbian couples frequently have less sex and intimacy than heterosexual couples.[89] Because women don't produce the same amount of natural testosterone as men—testosterone that drives sexual desire and brings a man and woman together—lesbian relationships often suffer from a lack of sex and intimacy. But don't be fooled into thinking that bed death only occurs in lesbian relationships. Heterosexual relationships often suffer from bed death as well. If you're passive and wait for a woman to make the first move, the woman will resent you and come to view you as weak and submissive. To arouse desire, you must abandon inhibition and throw yourself into sex with passion and gusto.

Men often worry that if they do this they'll offend a woman's delicate sensibilities. These men are quick to put a woman's needs first and make her pleasure their number one priority. The danger with this approach is that it does nothing to stimulate desire. As a man, your pleasure should be your number one priority.

You must take control of the interaction and lead a woman into the bedroom as though you can't wait to rip her clothes off and make love to her.

One of the most common complaints leveled against men is that men have become too passive and submissive in bed. They lack passion, refuse to take the lead, and the sex is often predictable and boring. There's no sense of danger or eroticism. If you make a woman feel as though she's there to serve you and give you pleasure, her enjoyment will come as a direct result of your pleasure. If you're in any doubt that sexually dominant behavior is desirable and attractive, you only have to look at movies like *Fifty Shades of Gray*, *9 ½ weeks*, and *Secretary* to see that women, by and large, are obsessed with the idea of dominance and submission.

A study carried out by researchers at Penn State University noted that women reported more regular, earlier-timed orgasms during sexual intercourse with men who were more masculine and dominant. Furthermore, the Penn State study also discovered that women experienced more frequent orgasms during or after a man's orgasm.[90] In other words, if you're enjoying the sexual experience, a woman is more likely to experience pleasure and orgasm as a direct result of your enjoyment. What turns you on? What makes you feel excited? Think about this for a moment. Once you know what you want in the bedroom, you must have the courage to go after your desires without inhibition. Sex doesn't have to be complicated; it just has to be fun.

Being sexually dominant doesn't mean you have to use whips and chains and wear a gimp suit. To be dominant, all that's required is your masculine presence. You come to the interaction with a "loaded gun," ready to engage in a dramatic encounter. As the woman waits for you, you can no longer contain yourself. You must have her even if it means ripping her clothes off and destroying her panties. This type of behavior, however, doesn't come naturally to nice guys, especially men who are trained from birth to hold women in high esteem and respect physical boundaries at all costs. As you become more dominant in the bedroom, there will be times when it feels as though you've crossed the line between what's acceptable and what's unacceptable. The attractive man, however, understands one simple truth: women crave controlled danger, they crave the attention of sexually dominant men, and they crave submission.

Sexual dominance, in this instance, is not about using force or aggression (although in some instances it can be). Sexual dominance is about letting a woman know what you want and having the courage to make her submit to you. It's important to note that sexual dominance is made up of two components: the physical and the verbal.

When it comes to physical dominance, let's imagine you're having sex in the missionary position. To display dominance, all you have to do is hold a woman's hands above her head or out to the side, pressing her down against the bed. In the same way, putting a woman's legs over your shoulders, forcing her into a more submissive position is another way to exert physical dominance. If you're having sex with a woman from behind, you can slap her on the butt (an act that drives women wild and makes them feel even more submissive). Additional ways to introduce dominance in the bedroom include twisting a woman's arm behind her back to force her into a more submissive position. Even when she's riding on top of you, in what is supposedly a dominant position for the woman, you can lightly pull her hair and slap her on the butt to make her feel even more submissive. Light hair pulling and soft choking is another way to force the woman into a state of submission and spike arousal.

When it comes to verbal dominance, telling a woman how much you want to fuck her is a sure way to drive her wild. For even the most prudish woman, dirty talk can be a wonderful aphrodisiac. Another important part of the dominant/submissive relationship is getting a woman to comply with your requests. When you tell a woman: "You love fucking me, don't you?" Most women will accept and internalize what you say. Even if the woman doesn't respond, it's of little importance. As you continue to engage the woman in sexual intercourse, you can introduce more dominant verbal language to intensify arousal. Simple, short commands often work best: "Don't stop." "Keep going." "Make me come." The more you get a woman to comply with your requests, the more submissive she's likely to become. If, for whatever reason, a woman refuses to submit, you must become more forceful and direct in your approach. If she continues to put up resistance, you must cut the interaction short and pull away as a form of punishment. You must never let a woman's resistance affect you for she's simply asking the question: are you man enough to make her submit?

NEVER GIVE YOUR LOVE TOO EASILY

There is a charm about the forbidden that makes it unspeakably desirable.

— Mark Twain

How long does it take a woman to fall in love? Research published in the *Journal of Social Psychology* found that out of 172 participants, it took men anywhere from a couple of days to a couple of weeks to fall in love; whereas women took no less than a couple of months to fall in love.[99] This is why you should never rush a woman into love and commitment. If you try to rush the seduction process, you're forcing a woman to feel emotions for you that she's not yet ready to feel. Your role as a man is to interact with a woman in a fun and relaxed way. Make no mistake, when a woman's ready to commit to you, she'll let you know. If you try to chase a woman into love and commitment (this includes talking about the relationship or trying to become exclusive), a woman will lose attraction for you and pull away.

Being a challenge is an important element of seduction that mustn't be forgotten. Less available men are, after all, viewed as more desirable romantic prospects. As stated in the *European Journal of Personality*, people who are less available are seen as having higher overall value even if that value is only perceived to be higher.[91] In business, if you tell a customer that a product has limited availability, your product immediately becomes more valuable as a result. If a woman looks at a diamond necklace in a shop window, she's most likely just browsing. Yet, if the same woman is told that this is the last diamond necklace of its kind in stock, there's a good chance the woman will be tempted to buy the necklace right there and then, such is the power of scarcity.[92] Playing hard to get requires a measure of strength and confidence, the same strength and confidence that women find attractive. The man who gives his love away too easily is like a cheap piece of jewelry—wanted by no one and often discarded.

LEAD HER INTO ATTRACTION

*A leader is one who knows the way,
goes the way, and shows the way.*

— Adam C. Maxwell

If there's one area of attraction where you can truly stand out and distinguish yourself, it's by taking the lead in the relationship. Men often fall short in this area because they don't understand what it means to lead a woman. They confuse the word *lead* with *control*—and a controlling man is the last thing a woman wants in her life. You must have the courage to give a woman freedom; at the same time, you must be able to lead a woman into attraction. As a man, your ultimate goal in any relationship should be to enjoy a woman's company as you lead her towards the bedroom. Sex, as crude as it might sound, is the ultimate destination for all male/female relationships. If this reality is subverted in favor of friendship, a woman will lose attraction for you and disappear from your life.

Leading a woman the right way is as simple as knowing what you want and having the courage to go after it. If you want to take a woman out on a date, your goal must be to have fun and seduce her. If you want to have sex with a woman, your goal must be to lead her towards intimacy. Leading doesn't have to be complicated, it only has to be done with confidence and a clear sense of purpose. A simple way to lead a woman is to ask yourself: what would you do if she wasn't with you? If you find yourself doing something that you wouldn't ordinarily do without her, then you know you're on the wrong path. Leading is doing what you want and letting the woman come along for the ride. Women by nature hate taking the lead in relationships. Once a woman takes the lead in the relationship, she'll inevitably start to feel as though she's the one in charge. This situation never sits well with women, and it's only a matter of time before they start to question your masculinity and confidence. From an evolutionary perspective, a man who's easily lead is easily taken advantage of, and thus more likely to be outwitted and outmatched by his opponents.

A study published in the journal *Human Nature* revealed that men who rate higher on indicators of social dominance and leadership are more attractive to women.[93] This is in sharp contrast to women who are rated more attractive when they score higher on indicators of submission and sensitivity. Another interesting aspect of this study was that dominant women were only rated attractive by other women (not men). This indicates that women find leadership qualities attractive regardless of a person's gender.

CASE STUDY #23: WOMEN SMELL WEAKNESS

Up until now, Lewis had been the perfect gentleman. This was only their third date and Lewis wanted Eva to know two things: one, he was a good guy; and two, he respected women. After they finished coffee, Eva smiled at Lewis and said she was hungry.

"Me too," Lewis replied.

"What do you want to eat?"

"I don't mind. I could eat anything."

"How about Italian?"

"Sounds great," Lewis said.

After sharing a large vegetarian pizza, Lewis made a conscious decision not to kiss Eva good night. That could wait. Why rush things and risk scaring her off?

When Eva got home, she felt confused. Lewis was obviously into her, but why did she feel like she was the one making all the decisions? Lewis had even agreed to share a large vegetarian pizza with her when he found out she was a pescatarian. And what was with that awkward, goodbye pat on the back he gave her when they said goodbye? That was weird. At that moment, Eva knew Lewis wasn't the right man for her. She needed someone who could make decisions and take the lead in the relationship. She needed someone who wasn't afraid to kiss her.

⅄

If you want to ask a woman out, you must do so without hesitation. If you want to kiss a woman, you must do so without apology. Far too many men are scared of offending women and hurting their feelings. In reality, a woman is more likely to be offended by a nice guy who's weak as opposed to a so-called "bad guy" who makes his intentions clear right from the start. Nice guys are paralyzed by anxiety, constantly asking themselves if it's okay to make a move? If it's okay to touch a woman? If it's okay to invite a woman back to their apartment? Maybe the woman will feel better if I let her make the decisions? After all, men and women are supposed to be equal, aren't they? These are just some of the ways nice guys self-sabotage and prevent themselves from taking the lead in relationships.

Leading a woman and being dominant is not, however, the same as being aggressive. You don't lead a woman by strong-arming her into following you. You don't use force or threats to gain compliance; in fact, doing so would only undermine your value. Research conducted by Pennsylvania State University noted that men who are playful, humorous, and fun to be around are considered more attractive and alluring.[94] The theory as to why these playful qualities are so endearing is that playful men are seen as more grounded, stable, and resilient when facing life's challenges and setbacks. Playful men are also perceived to be less aggressive and less likely to hurt a woman and her future offspring. Furthermore, these qualities are seen as a marker of social intelligence and indicate that a man can form faster social bonds with others thus increasing his ability to acquire more resources and protection from society. From an evolutionary perspective, this ties in with the theory that playful men are viewed as mentally strong and resilient. You should never confuse the qualities of dominance and assertiveness with aggression and anti-social behavior—two traits common to insecure men.

Even if a woman refuses to follow your lead, it's important not to get upset or derailed by her resistance. Being a leader doesn't mean being headstrong and stubborn. If you tell a woman you want to eat steak and she says no, simply ask her what she feels like eating instead. If she comes up with a better alternative that you're happy to go along with, there's no reason not to be flexible. Nevertheless, if she can't come up with a better alternative simply tell her you're going to eat steak and she's welcome to join you. In leadership, the person who has the strongest and clearest image of what they want prevails. You must never get upset or angry if a woman doesn't want to listen to you or follow your lead, you know what you want and that's all that counts. An attractive man does what he wants, whether a woman is willing to follow him or not.

PART FOUR

MAINTAIN ATTRACTION

*Even cowards can endure hardship;
only the brave can endure suspense.*

— Mignon McLaughlin

If you're only interested in short-term relationships, there's no need to worry about maintaining attraction over a long period of time. In brief encounters, all that's required is the initial spark of attraction to catch a woman's attention and seduce her. On the other hand, if you want to maintain a long-term relationship, you must know how to keep the fires of attraction alive, not just now, but over the course of many years. One reason why the divorce rate is currently so high (over 50 percent in developed countries) and the reason why women initiate the majority of divorces (approximately 70 percent) is that women often lose attraction for their husbands and see no alternative but to end the relationship.

CASE STUDY #24: "HE CHANGED"

Ben used to be a player. He knew all the pickup lines and he knew exactly where, when, and how to meet women and seduce them. He was so good at seducing women, in fact, that he always had three to five girls in his life at any one time. And right now, Ben was seeing Michelle, Kate, and Irene at various times throughout the week.

As far as Ben was concerned, Irene was just another girl in a long line of conquests. At least that was how he felt about her in the beginning. It wasn't long, however, before Ben started to pay more attention to Irene. She was different to all the other girls. She was sexy, beautiful, ambitious, and interesting. She was also fantastic in bed, and she let Ben do things to her that most men could only dream about. It wasn't long before Ben was spending more time with Irene and less time with Michelle and Kate.

A month later, Ben decided to focus exclusively on Irene. He had just turned 38, and Ben felt it was time to have a serious relationship after so many years fooling around.

* * *

Twelve months later, Ben and Irene were married with a baby on the way. Now only a month into the marriage, Ben was already starting to see the cracks appear in their relationship. For one, he had noticed that Irene was becoming increasingly bitchy and disrespectful towards him. On a number of occasions, she had even told him she couldn't stand the sight of him. At first, Ben thought she was joking; it turned out, she wasn't. On another occasion, Irene had gone so far as to call Ben a "stupid bitch." Where was all this animosity and hatred coming from? Ben closed his eyes and thought back to a time when Irene had wrapped her arms around him and told him how much she loved him. God, he missed those days.

Now that Irene was pregnant, it was clear that she was starting to lose interest in Ben. Irene didn't know what was wrong with her, but she knew her feelings towards Ben had changed. She wondered if her bitchiness might be caused by prenatal depression or the stress of being pregnant.

The moment they tied the knot, Ben had made the marriage his number one priority. He was always going out of his way to make her happy, and he was constantly telling her how much he loved her. He even bought Irene a new house as a sign of love and devotion to her and their unborn child. Despite all this, whenever Irene looked at Ben she felt nothing but disappointment bordering on contempt.

One night, in a moment of calm serenity, Irene told Ben she was trying to figure out what was wrong with her and she needed space and time to process her thoughts and feelings. Ben didn't like the sound of that—*space?* He told Irene there was no way he could leave her alone, especially when she was pregnant.

Over the next couple of weeks, Irene became increasingly irate as Ben tried his best to fix the relationship. Then, one morning, Irene woke up, and with perfect clarity knew what she had to do. She got into her car, drove to the clinic, and had an abortion. Irene wanted nothing more to do with Ben. In fact, the very sight of him made her feel sick. He wasn't the man she had fallen in love with. It was his fault, not hers. In the beginning, she had relished the occasional moments of attention he had given her. She knew he was seeing other women, but she found the challenge of winning him over both thrilling and exciting. It wasn't until later that Irene came to realize how much Ben had changed. If she had a craving for chocolate, Ben would run to the store and buy her chocolate. If she disagreed with him, he would instantly back down and try to please her. What happened to the man she had fallen in love with? Now Irene couldn't look at Ben without feeling a sense of regret. His weakness was palpable. Irene felt as though she no longer had any time to herself and whenever she needed space, Ben was always there, hanging around in the background like a bad smell. Irene knew she now had no choice but to get out of the relationship as fast as possible.

A

In the early stages of a relationship, the connection is still fresh and invigorating. Then, over the course of time, the man starts to soften. He lets his guard down and becomes sweeter and more responsive to the woman's needs. This works for a time, perhaps a couple of weeks, perhaps a couple of months, then, out of nowhere, the woman becomes increasingly withdrawn and difficult to deal with. For her part, the woman has no idea why she's feeling so ambivalent about the relationship, the only thing she knows for sure is that she no longer feels the same way. She wants out, and the relationship as far as the woman is concerned is dead.

This section is all about maintaining attraction. If you want to keep attraction alive in a long-term relationship, you need to know how to handle problems when they arise and you need to know how to maintain attraction over an extended period of time, keeping the fires of attraction alive through the good times and the bad.

STAY LIGHT AND RELAXED

*Never, ever underestimate the
importance of having fun.*

— Randy Pausch

Whether you're in the early stages of a relationship or a ten-year marriage, it's crucial to keep your relationships light and fun if you want to maintain attraction. Most men enter relationships with the end goal already in sight—final destination: marriage and kids. Using all their powers of deductive reasoning, men often assume that in order to get from point (a) where they currently are to point (b) marriage and kids, they must focus on the relationship and do everything they can to make a woman fall in love with them. The moment you become too serious and relationship focused, however, is the moment you kill attraction and risk turning your partner off.

CASE STUDY #25: WHY SO SERIOUS?

Helen was dating both Marty and Ryan at the same time. And so far, there'd been no intimacy, no sex, and only a couple of dates with both men. Helen hoped she would develop feelings for either Marty or Ryan at some point in time, making it easier to choose one man over the other. Up until now, however, Helen was still finding it hard to choose between the two men. In terms of looks, Marty was definitely the physically more attractive man. He was in great shape, tall, and naturally handsome. Ryan, on the other hand, was average looking at best.

One day, when Helen was getting ready to see Marty, she thought back to their previous date and remembered how handsome Marty had looked sitting there in the dark, candlelit restaurant—handsome until he had opened his mouth and started complaining about everything and everyone. At first, Helen found it easy to empathize with Marty and she encouraged him to talk more openly about his problems. After all, she had faced similar problems at work, and she knew what it was like to be around colleagues who didn't appreciate you.

For the next couple of hours, Marty and Helen swapped horror stories. Marty told Helen how his parents had failed to support him in college and how they had "forced him" to change his major from film and television—his one true passion—to business. Again, Helen sympathized with Marty. She remembered how she had wanted to study fashion in college, but her parents had persuaded her to study accounting instead. As Marty gazed across the table, his eyes began to tear. Finally, here was a woman who understood him.

It was only when she got home that Helen began to realize how negative Marty was. She thought about Ryan. He was so different to Marty. He didn't have a care in the world. He never spoke about the past and never worried about the future. It was as though all he wanted to do in life was have fun. Sure, he wasn't as handsome as Marty, but his positive, playful attitude more than made up for it. It was at that moment that Helen realized which man she wanted to be with.

⅄

Mindfulness is the ability to focus on the present without worrying about the past or the future. A study published in the *Journal of Personality and Individual Differences* discovered that mindful men were rated more attractive compared to non-mindful men.[95] In the study, male participants were asked to fill out a mindfulness questionnaire where they were asked to rate themselves on statements like: "I perceive my feelings and emotions without having to react to them." Men who were aware of their emotions, but didn't allow their emotions to overwhelm them were labeled more mindful. It was also found that mindful men demonstrated a greater ability to stay focused on the present. Mindful personality traits are attractive to women because men who present a mindful disposition are also more likely to rate higher on mental strength and confidence.

A recent study published by researchers at California State University, Long Beach noted how playfulness, which means having a "sense of humor," and the ability to have fun and maintain a playful attitude is one of the most attractive qualities a man can have.[96] A further study carried out by researchers at Stanford University School of Medicine observed that women enjoy being in the presence of men who can make them laugh.[97] The study found that a woman's biological reward circuitry is wired to respond more positively to humor than men. Men, on the other hand, are more likely to respond to inspiring and positive messages. In the Stanford University experiment, the male and female participants were asked to view funny video clips (showing people falling over and animals performing tricks). The same participants were then asked to watch positive videos (that consisted of videos of dancers and snowboarders). When viewing the funny videos, the women showed greater activity in the midbrain and amygdala regions compared to men when viewing the same funny videos. This explains why humor is so attractive to women from a biological perspective.

Research continues to show that women are attracted to men who are humorous and can make them laugh. Humor, for one, is seen as a significant marker of intelligence. One study published in *Psychological Reports* had three men sit at a bar near other female patrons.[98] In the first experiment, two men listened as another man told a joke. The man who told the joke was then instructed to approach a woman sitting close by and ask for her number. In the second experiment, again, two men listened as another man told a joke. Only this time, the researchers instructed one of the listeners, not the joke teller, to approach a nearby woman and ask the woman for her number. This situation was repeated approximately sixty times at different times and locations to ensure that the results of the experiment remained valid. At the end of the experiment, the researchers found that the man who told the joke and displayed obvious signs of humor was three times more likely to get a woman's number compared to the man who had just listened to the joke. The researchers then asked the women to rate the men on their overall level of attractiveness. The results showed that the man who told the joke before approaching the woman was rated much more attractive and intelligent than the man who had simply listened to the joke.

The results of the study are fascinating because they show just how important it is for men to display humor and the important role that humor plays in attraction. Humor also sends the signal that a man has social dexterity and a mindful disposition. This is why it's so important to remain light and playful in your relationships.

DON'T FOCUS ON
THE RELATIONSHIP

Talking about relationships is a
surefire way to jinx them.

— Maggie Grace

In all relationships, men and women have assigned gender roles. These gender roles are not assigned by society or culture, they're assigned by nature. If a woman believes she must take the lead in the relationship, she's being forced to act in a way that runs contrary to her nature. The same applies to men who seek commitment and focus on the relationship— they, too, are behaving in a way that runs contrary to their nature. The relationship-focused man kills attraction because his behavior is feminine. And as research published in the *Personality and Social Psychology Bulletin* explains: men who are too caring and relationship focused are rated less attractive by women.[99] Highly responsive men believe that if they talk about their feelings, they'll be able to form a strong connection with a woman and get her to fall in love with them. They believe that affirmations of love will make the woman feel more secure in the relationship. In reality, anytime you're too responsive, putting relationships at the forefront of your life, you risk killing attraction. Responsiveness, as measured by researchers, encompasses a series of traits that includes being nurturing, kind, supportive, and emotionally available. Surprisingly, and somewhat counter-intuitively, these responsive traits have been found to kill attraction and turn women off.

CASE STUDY #26: NEVER SEEK LOVE TO GET LOVE

Kate and Doug had just had finished making love for the first time. As they lay next to each other, all hot and sweaty, Doug reached over and touched Kate on the arm. "That was amazing."

"I hope you don't think we're in a relationship," Kate said as she pulled away from him.

"Why'd you say that?" Doug said, taken aback. "Why'd you sleep with me then?"

"I'm just not ready for a relationship," Kate said as she slipped out of bed and got dressed. Doug had no idea that this was the first and last time he would ever have sex with Kate. His desperate, needy behavior would ultimately destroy what little attraction Kate had left for him.

* * *

Six months later, Kate and Eddie had just finished making love for the first time. As they lay in bed, all hot and sweaty, Eddie reached over and touched Kate on the arm. "That was awesome."

"Just so you know, I'm not looking for a relationship," Kate said.

"Why would I want a relationship?" Eddie replied.

"I'm just letting you know."

"Take it easy. We've only just met." Eddie said as he jumped out of bed. Kate took a deep breath and relaxed. She felt relief, especially after her last experience with Doug. Little did Kate realize that two months from now she would be on the phone with her best friend, crying because Eddie refused to commit to her.

⅄

When a woman thinks you're overly focused on the relationship and emotionally affected by everything she does, she'll naturally start to question your masculinity. The woman's natural instinct is to then pull away and study your behavior from a distance.

Take the following situations as an example: (1) A woman has sex with a man without expressing any emotion or feeling for him and the man gets upset; (2) A woman can't see her boyfriend on Valentine's day and the man responds by throwing a tantrum; (3) The man confuses feelings of lust for love and tells his girlfriend that he's falling in love with her on the third date.

In all three situations, the man is overly focused on the relationship. To protect yourself from situations like this, you must take the focus off the relationship. Women are relationship focused; men are mission focused. The moment you subvert this natural dynamic is the moment you kill attraction by focusing on the woman when you should be focusing on yourself instead.

GIVE HER WHAT SHE NEEDS

*What I like and what I need's
two different things.*

— J.D. Jordan

A woman asks for commitment, love, and devotion and a man thinks if he gives her these things he'll make her happy. He takes the woman's words at face value only to discover later that when he gives the woman what she asked for she pulls away from him and starts to lose interest. Why does this happen and why do women punish men for giving them what they want?

CASE STUDY #27: SHE WANTED MORE LOVE

"I need you to show me more love," Jen said right after Eddie told her he was going fishing on the weekend. Over the course of their ten-year marriage, Eddie thought he had done a pretty good job of showing Jen how much he loved her.

"I need to feel like you care about me. And I need to feel like I can trust you. I don't know what you get up to when you go on these 'fishing trips' with your buddies," Jen said.

"Oh, honey, I just go fishing that's all."

"How do I know? You could be doing anything. Anyway, I'm just saying I need to feel like you actually care about me."

"Of course, I care about you, come on," Eddie said. "Tell you what, I'll cancel my fishing trip and we can spend the weekend together. Just you and me. How's that sound?"

"You'd do that for me?" Jen said, all wide-eyed and innocent.

"Of course, I would," Eddie replied. Five minutes later, Eddie called up his buddies and canceled the fishing trip.

"Why'd you cancel?" Jen asked.

"I thought you wanted to spend the weekend together."

"You didn't have to cancel your fishing trip."

"What are you talking about?"

"I said you didn't have to cancel."

"Are you serious?" Eddie didn't know what to say. Jen was the one who said she wanted more love and attention. Now, after giving her exactly what she asked for, she was getting all bitchy about it. In fact, she had been downright nasty ever since he had canceled the trip.

When the weekend finally arrived, Jen told Eddie she now wanted to spend the weekend by herself. WTF? Eddie tried to protest, but Jen cut him off. It didn't make any sense. He had given her what she wanted and now she was punishing him for it.

᠕

A woman might tell you she needs more love and attention. She might even tell you that she wants a man who's honest and faithful. And at other times, she might tell you that all she wants is to feel safe and secure. It's important, in all of these situations, not to focus on what a woman says she *wants* but to instead focus on what she *needs*. Will giving a woman more attention make her feel more attracted to you? Will giving a woman a sense of safety and security make you more attractive as a man? Does going out of your way to be true, honest, and faithful make a woman want you more? The answer to all of these questions is a resounding *no*.

There are few occasions in life where giving a woman what she wants will make her feel heightened levels of attraction for you. When you give a woman what she asks for, she's more likely to resent you for giving in to her demands. The moment you give a woman what she wants is the moment she starts to lose respect for you. This might not happen straight away. The woman might, in fact, respond positively to your compliance at first. But once the woman comes to realize that you're willing to change your behavior just to please her, she'll come to resent you for your weakness and pliability.

You'll often hear jilted men scream in frustration: "What about me? I gave you everything you asked for. I was there for you and I loved you with all my heart. No other guy will love you like I do or care about you the same way." What these men fail to realize is that women aren't looking for men to give them what they *want*, they're looking for men to give them what they *need*. Given a choice between the two, a woman will always choose to be with the man who gives her what she needs.

When you're with a woman, you must pay careful

attention to her behavior. If a woman tells you that she's changed her mind about the relationship and now just wants to be friends, it's tempting to take the woman's words at face value and believe what she says. Another example is when a woman pulls out the ever-present, yet well-worn cliché: "I'm not looking for a relationship, I just want to hang out." Once again, the temptation is to acquiesce and take the woman's words at face value. Of course, women don't just want to be friends; they need sex and intimacy like everyone else. It's your job to give a woman what she needs, not what she wants. This is a lot easier to do when you ask yourself one simple question: what is the strongest course of action I can take?

A woman might tell you that she'll cut you off and punish you for not listening to her, or for not giving in to her demands, but you mustn't let her threats affect you or derail you because you understand one vital truth: when you exhibit strength, she will always come back. Few men can remain strong and resilient in the face of a woman's demands—you must be the exception.

DON'T PLAY IT SAFE

*A ship in port is safe, but that's
not what ships are built for.*

— John A. Shedd

When it comes to life and relationships, most men like to play it safe. This playing it safe strategy includes a reluctance to upset women. If you want to create any real, lasting attraction with women, however, you must be able to venture out of your comfort zone and endure a certain degree of discomfort and pain. Attraction, after all, doesn't grow in safety and security, attraction grows in a swamp of anxiety, fear, jealousy, anger, and sadness. All the negative emotions we try so hard to avoid in daily life are, in fact, the same emotions you must embrace if you want to build attraction with women.

CASE STUDY #28: POLARIZE HER EMOTIONS

Rick and Heather were out having dinner when Rick told Heather he was going to use the rest of his savings—approximately $15,000—to restore an old '66 Mustang convertible.

Heather paused for a moment. "Are you serious?"

"It's gonna look amazing," Rick said. "I mean, it's not cheap, but it's totally worth it." Heather's look said it all—she wasn't impressed. "What is it, what's wrong?" Rick said, chewing his food.

"Why don't you just buy a new one instead of an old rust bucket," Heather replied. Heather was known for her sharp tongue and tonight was no exception.

"What?" Rick said. "Because it's vintage. They don't make 'em anymore."

"There's a reason they stopped making them," Heather replied.

"Look, it's a '66 Mustang."

"I can't believe I'm dating an idiot," Heather groaned.

"Come on," Rick said.

"It's stupid."

"Don't be like that."

"Idiot," Heather hissed.

Without saying another word, Rick reached across the table and knocked Heather's glass of wine over. The wine spilled across the table onto Heather's lap. "That's for being a bitch," Rick said, dabbing his mouth with a napkin.

Heather was too shocked to respond. She shook her head, stumbled to her feet, then ran out of the restaurant. Rick didn't care. He was only too happy to get rid of her.

* * *

When Heather got home she was still crying. She had never felt so angry or humiliated in her entire life. She stepped out of her wine-soaked dress and jumped in the shower. The water felt wonderful. Heather stood under the shower, letting the hot water wash over her body. Then, for some inexplicable reason, she began to laugh. She couldn't help it. Rick might be a rude son of a bitch, but he was definitely an improvement on her last boyfriend, Eric. Heather must have called Eric "stupid" more than a thousand times over the course of their relationship, and all he ever did was apologize and say sorry. As the years went by, Heather grew more and more disgusted by Eric's behavior. She closed her eyes, letting the heat from the water soak into her skin. At least Rick knows how to stand up for himself. Come to think of it, he's pretty damn sexy when he's mad. The moment Heather stepped out of the shower, she grabbed her phone and called Rick's number.

⅄

Modern culture states that peoples' emotions are sacred territory. We must never hurt another person's feelings or upset them in any way. Nonetheless, if you go through life reluctant to upset a woman or disturb her sense of tranquility, you'll have little to no impact on a woman's feelings or emotions. And if a woman feels nothing for you, she'll lose interest in you and focus her attention elsewhere. Women need to feel their emotions because emotions are the centerpiece of a woman's life.

Every human interaction is laced with emotion. These emotions can either be on the positive side of the spectrum such as sex, pleasure, affection, warmth, and love, or these emotions can be on the negative side of the spectrum such as jealousy, anger, sadness, and fear. Women are feeling creatures who are driven by their emotions. If a woman is in a relationship with a man who inspires strong emotions, whether those emotions are positive or negative, the woman is more likely to focus on the man and fall under his spell.

Research into attraction discovered that women are attracted to men who inspire feelings of anxiety and uncertainty. But that one question still remains to be answered: why are women more attracted to men who make them feel anxious and uncertain? A study carried out by the University of Chicago finally shed light on this question when researchers reported that people are much more likely to work hard and pay a "higher price" for a reward when the reward is "uncertain" as opposed to "known." The researchers in the study noted that people are often pushed harder by the fantasy of "winning big" in much the same way that people are enthralled by the prospect of winning the lottery.[100]

Human beings are driven by hope and the knowledge that it's possible to get what we want, even if the odds are stacked against us. As humans, we have an insatiable desire to bring order and control into our lives by "resolving the uncertain" and bringing the "unknown into the light of understanding." Once we come to understand and appreciate this aspect of human nature, it's possible to see how feelings of anxiety can have such a profound and dramatic effect on the human condition. Of course, anxiety is by no means a positive emotion for women to experience, but anxiety does without doubt build attraction by focusing a woman's attention on the source of her discomfort—*you*.

There's no point trying to make a woman feel good all the time. That would be an exercise in futility. Yes, there will be extended periods of bliss, but make no mistake, relationships often give birth to extended periods of discomfort and anxiety. You must be able to weather a woman's chaotic emotions whenever they surface, and indeed, create your own storms to ensure you remain at the forefront of a woman's mind. You should never attempt to play it safe with women. If your goal is to spark attraction and maintain interest over the long-run, you must allow a woman to feel angry, sad, bitter, frustrated, nervous, anxious, resentful, jealous, envious, and disappointed. Only then, can you expect to grab a woman's attention and inspire the kind of attraction that most men can only dream about.

ANXIETY FUELS ATTRACTION

Women are more attracted to men who put them into a fearful and anxious state.

— Archives of Sexual Behavior

According to a study published in the journal *Psychological Science* titled "He Loves Me, He Loves Me Not... Uncertainty Can Increase Romantic Attraction," anxiety has been shown to increase a woman's attraction for a man.[101] These days, it's often more beneficial for a man to bring a sense of anxiety and uncertainty into a relationship with a women as opposed to bringing a sense of security and certainty. Women, of course, don't enjoy being thrust into a state of anxiety. But results are what count here, and research shows that women feel heightened levels of attraction for men when they feel anxious. Again, it's not our concern whether this is unethical or immoral, it's simply a matter of knowing what women respond to and what actions get results.

Women don't respond to safety and security with happiness, loyalty, and affection. In reality, when a woman feels safe and secure she's more likely to pull away, create unnecessary drama, get bored, and lose interest.[102] To grab a woman's attention, you must first give the impression that a relationship is the last thing on your mind. If a woman has to fight to be in a relationship with you, she'll find you even more irresistible and charming.

Numerous psychological studies show that objects and people are perceived to be more desirable and attractive when in limited supply. This is the same reason why people covet diamonds—a mineral perceived to have limited availability. If diamonds were in abundance, people would no longer spend thousands of dollars to acquire them. The same concept applies to relationships. If you actively seek love from women and try to make a woman feel safe and secure, you send the signal that your love has little value because it's easily acquired. You instill neither anxiety nor scarcity, and as a result, your value as a romantic prospect is greatly diminished.

YOUR LOVER IS NOT YOUR MOTHER

I'm not your mother, so get off my tit.

— Unknown

Women by design have *hypergamous* natures. This means that women are hard-wired to mate with men they view as superior to themselves. Hypergamy also states that if a woman senses weakness in a man, she'll look to fill the void with another man of superior strength. Hypergamy is one of the main reasons why women cheat on their partners. And when you understand the concept of hypergamy, it's no longer a surprise that a study found that approximately one out of every twenty-five fathers are biologically unrelated to their children.[103] Hypergamy is the reason why you must be eternally vigilant around women.

When you view women through the prism of your own relationship with your mother, it's easy to assume that all women are kind and supportive. The truth is, it's impossible for a woman to love you in the same way your mother loves you. You are your mother's flesh and blood. When your mother looks at you, she sees herself. You are as much a part of her as she is a part of you. Part of the reason why men assume that women are such sweet, loving creatures is that their own mothers have always been so devoted and loving towards them. Therefore, it stands to reason that every woman must be the same. And it's true, all women do have the same emotional capacity for love, but that unconditional love won't be directed towards you; instead, a woman's unconditional love is saved exclusively for her children.

Any man who's experienced the sudden withdrawal of a once sweet, loving girlfriend or wife knows that a woman's love isn't unconditional. Far too many men make the mistake of treating their girlfriends and wives like a substitute mother. They believe their partner will always be there for them. After all, their mothers were always there for them and would forgive them no matter what. Therefore, it stands to reason that all women must be the same. The moment you start treating your lover like your mother is the moment your lover starts looking for someone else to love.

NEVER FOLLOW A WOMAN'S LEAD

Only one man in a 1000 is a leader of men—the other 999 follow women.

— Groucho Marx

Sometimes a woman will try to suck you into a relationship as fast as possible. From day one, she's intense and passionate. And by the end of the week, she's telling you how much she loves you. When this happens, it's tempting to try and match the woman's intensity with the same level of passion. And why not? She's into you and obviously loves being around you. It's at times like this that you must consciously hold back and resist being drawn in by the woman's intensity.

If you tell a woman that you love her too soon, you risk lowering your value and derailing the seduction process. The woman, having started out with such intensity, will eventually come to realize that the relationship is moving too fast and that she doesn't, in fact, love you. She was just in love with the idea of being in love. And even though it was the woman who pursued you in the first place, it's your fault for rushing the seduction. If you allow yourself to be pulled in by a woman too soon, don't be surprised if the relationship disintegrates and falls apart with the same speed with which it materialized.

Similarly, when a woman says she wants to go to the ballet or go shopping, most men will jump at the opportunity to accompany the woman. For the great majority of men, it doesn't matter if they enjoy the ballet or not, what matters is the opportunity—the opportunity to be with a woman and the opportunity to have sex with her. Women understand that most men have no interest in going shopping or spending a night at the ballet. The moment you willingly trade comfort for sex is the moment you become vulnerable and start to look weak.

CASE STUDY #29: LAMB TO THE SLAUGHTER

Around 11 p.m. on Friday night, Scott received a message from Janice: *"Just at Skybar with a friend. Come join us!"* Ever since he had first met Janice a couple of weeks ago, Scott had found himself thinking about her more times than he cared to admit. Deep down, Scott wanted nothing more than to go to sleep, but he knew this was a golden opportunity to see Janice and possibly have sex with her. It was Friday night after all.

* * *

When Scott arrived at the bar an hour later, he saw Janice standing in the VIP area with a group of friends. Scott didn't expect to see Janice with so many people, he thought she was just going to be hanging out with her friend Kelsey. Scott approached the group and tapped Janice on the shoulder.

"Scott, you made it!" Janice shrieked, throwing her arms around him. "Let me introduce you to everyone."

"Can't wait," Scott said, trying his best to feign interest.

An hour later, Scott found himself standing on the edge of the group, talking to a guy called Mike who, it turns out, was also there to see Janice. Janice, meanwhile, continued to ignore Scott. He had tried talking to her a couple of times, but she didn't seem that interested in anything he had to say.

"I knew coming here was a big mistake," Scott muttered as he went to the bar to order another drink. By the time he came back, Scott was just in time to see Janice and Kelsey say good night to everyone. What a colossal waste of time, Scott thought. I should've just gone to bed. At least then I would still have a chance with this girl instead of looking like a total loser.

⅄

When you allow a woman to put you in situations that undermine your comfort and control, you inadvertently kill attraction by letting her know that you're willing to sacrifice happiness and comfort just to bathe in her presence. All you have to do is listen to your instincts. The moment a woman asks you to do something that's inconvenient or doesn't feel right—refuse. Never be afraid to make yourself unavailable for the attractive man understands one fundamental rule: attraction grows in space. A woman will always test you to see if she can hold power over you. This includes canceling dates, asking you to go out of your way to meet her, as well as trying to get you to drop whatever it is you're doing for no good reason. The weak man bends to a woman's will; the attractive man marches to the beat of his own drum.

BUYING GIFTS FOR WOMEN

*It irritates the hell out of me,
but you can't buy love.*

— Warren Buffett

The best gift you can buy a woman is, surprisingly, no gift at all. If you think you can buy a woman's love you're deluding yourself. And while it is sometimes possible to get a woman to spend time with you if you spend enough money on her, it's important to make a distinction between a woman who's with you because she's attracted to you and a woman who's with you because she loves your money and the lifestyle you can provide.

At a biological level, it's true that women desire men who have resources, or at least the ability to acquire resources. A detailed study of beauty and status published in the *American Sociological Review* highlights the fact that although women do exchange beauty for status, the most attractive character trait is a man's ability to acquire resources, not the resources themselves.[104] The wealthy man who inherits a fortune does little to attract women. On the other hand, the self-made man is attractive because his determination and drive is a testament to his character and mental strength.

Since the dawn of romanticism in the late 18th century, men have conditioned themselves to believe that acting in a romantic way results in heightened levels of love and attraction. To this day, modern romantics continue to provide women with an endless supply of gifts, art, poetry, and literature all in an effort to win a woman over and capture her interest. Romanticism is so prolific that entire industries have sprung up to support its cause. Valentine's day, anniversaries, Christmas day, New Year's Eve, and birthdays are now all cause for romantic celebration, leaving the modern man with a sense of obligation to declare his love as often and as frequently as possible. As a result, men have come to expect declarations of love and devotion from women in return.

CASE STUDY #30: EXPECTATION & DISCONTENT

Every Valentine's day for the last three years, Luke went out and bought Jess a bouquet of flowers and a box of chocolates. This Valentine's day was no exception. Only this year the unexpected happened. When Luke gave Jess her Valentine's present, Jess apologized and told Luke that she had completely forgotten what day it was. Luke smiled and told Jess it was no big deal and nothing to worry about.

Later that evening, during a romantic candlelit dinner, Luke barely said a word until after he had finished his meal. It was then that Luke took a deep breath and told Jess he needed to get something off his chest. He proceeded to tell Jess how much she had hurt his feelings. Valentine's day was a tradition, a tradition they'd kept alive for four years and it was an important milestone in their relationship. Again, Jess apologized and told Luke how much she loved him.

Unfortunately for Jess, her declaration of love wasn't enough to calm Luke's nerves. I can't believe this, Luke thought. I've given her so much, bought her gifts, booked and paid for dinner, and she can't even remember what day it is.

As they drove home, Luke continued to berate Jess for ruining such a special day. Jess put her head against the passenger side window and closed her eyes. She wished he would just shut up and get over it. How many more times did she have to listen to him complain about the same thing over and over again?

* * *

Later that night, as Luke and Jess lay next to each other, Luke tried to kiss Jess on the lips to bridge the distance between them.

"Are you okay?" Luke asked.

A minute passed before Jess rolled over and told Luke she wasn't in the mood to have sex, not tonight. Jess excused herself and went to the bathroom. When she came back she was shocked to see Luke curled up on the side of the bed, crying. "What's wrong?" Jess whispered.

"You don't love me anymore," Luke replied as he tried to fight back the tears.

Jess moved towards the bed, about to comfort Luke, when something stopped her. It was as though someone had just shone a light onto her boyfriend and exposed him for what he was—an emotionally weak and fragile man.

* * *

Twelve months later, Luke was gone and Jess was now dating a guy called Mike. With Valentine's day fast approaching, Jess thought back to the previous year and what a disaster it had been. Jess had never known how weak and insecure Luke was until that moment. Now she knew what signs to look out for she wasn't about to make the same mistake again. This year, Jess had made a conscious decision not to buy Mike anything for Valentine's day. She wanted to see how Mike would respond. Would he get upset like Luke or would he pass her test?

When Valentine's day finally arrived, Jess called Mike and invited him out for dinner. Mike surprised Jess by telling her he couldn't make it because he had other plans. Jess took a moment to compose herself. She reminded Mike that today was a "special day," but Mike had no idea what she was talking about.

"It's Valentine's day," Jess said.

"Sorry, babe, I had no idea. But I can't make it today. I'll make it up to you later." Jess began to protest, but Mike cut her off mid-sentence by telling her that Valentine's day was "just another day."

When Mike hung up the phone, Jess couldn't help but smile. Somehow she felt relieved. It's a shame she couldn't see Mike tonight, she missed him already.

⚓

An attractive man doesn't rely on gimmicks and gifts to lure a woman into his life because he knows his presence is the gift, not the Tiffany necklace. Only the weak and insecure man feels the need to buy gifts in a desperate attempt to win a woman's approval. The only time you should consider buying gifts for women is not, as is commonly thought, on typical gift-giving days like birthdays, Christmas day, Valentine's day, and anniversaries, but on those occasions where a woman deserves it and least expects it. An unexpected gift is much more appreciated and valued for it is received with surprise and gratitude and never taken for granted.

ATTRACTION GROWS IN SPACE

Eroticism resides in the ambiguous space
between anxiety and fascination.

— Esther Perel

If there's one area of attraction that mustn't be ignored, it's the concept of space. Space, or a lack of space, is responsible for more breakups than just about any other relationship problem. Space is so powerful and important it is, in essence, the means by which attraction either thrives or dies. Men and women are born into the world as single entities. The moment we come out of our mother's womb, we start to develop a sense of self and a sense of our own individual identity. We begin to separate ourselves from our parents as we come to see ourselves as unique individual beings separate from other people and the world around us. This separation of self drives our need for space. We need space to grow. We need space to develop. We need space to think. And we need space to have a sense of our own individual identity.

In most relationships, when two people come together, the concept of space is usually forgotten. Most relationships start with a bang. The man and woman come together with passion, frequently "love bombing" the other person, only to discover later that they've squeezed all the life out of the relationship.

This is the great paradox of space—we want to be free and separate from others, yet we also desire closeness and connection at the same time. Introducing space is not only important in the early stages of a relationship where coming on too strong can have disastrous consequences. Space must also be present in long-term relationships as well. When a woman loses attraction for a man, it's usually because the man failed to bring enough space and distance into the relationship. In the same way, when a woman loses interest in sex, it's usually because she feels deprived of space, and as a result, her attraction has begun to fade.

Attraction doesn't grow in close proximity, it grows in space. When space is introduced, the focus comes off the self and back on to the other. When we feel suffocated in a relationship, this is because the focus is on the other as opposed to the self. Only when our partner grants us space do we crave intimacy and turn our attention back to our partner. This is a cycle that all healthy relationships must strive to balance, a balance that is often hard to accomplish if one person requires more intimacy than the other.

People who are insecure, lonely, or have a personality type that makes them feel anxious often oppose the idea of space, preferring instead to live in a co-dependent relationship. For the vast majority of people, introducing space shouldn't be a problem. Most people have a secure attachment style (approximately 59 percent of the population); 25 percent of people have an avoidant attachment style that requires fewer close connections and a reduced need for intimacy; and 11 percent of people have an anxious attachment style that lends itself to feelings of insecurity, anxiety, and the fear that their partner will one day abandon them. Regardless of a person's attachment style, you must always allow space into your relationships, even if it feels like space is the last thing the relationship needs.

In Esther Perel's *Mating in Captivity,* eroticism and sexual attraction are said to exist in an ambiguous zone between anxiety and fascination.[105] The amount of attraction (sexual or otherwise) we feel for another person is often in direct proportion to the amount of anxiety and uncertainty the other person stirs within us. The moment a woman feels smothered in a relationship is the moment she begins to feel a slew of emotions ranging from boredom, apathy, suffocation, and restlessness. On the other hand, the moment the all-important element of space is introduced, the woman is no longer assured of the man's presence. It's at this point that the woman begins to feel anxious and excited, becoming more and more fixated on the man the longer he's away from her.

Whether you find yourself in a new relationship or a twenty-year marriage, you must learn to embrace space and welcome it into your life. In the same way, you must resist the natural temptation to close the distance between you and your lover. Men are often plagued by the thought that a woman will forget about them, or, worse, find someone else and move on the moment space is introduced. Just as your ability to introduce anxiety into a relationship is often commensurate with the amount of attraction a woman feels for you, your ability to introduce space is also a direct reflection of your mental strength and character. There's nothing more terrifying for a woman than the prospect of losing her freedom and being trapped within the confines of a suffocating relationship. Of all the values we hold dear, freedom is the most important. Yes, we must eat and breathe to survive, but without freedom we lose our humanity and the will to live. This is true of all animals, not just humans. Only an insecure man would deny a woman space in a desperate attempt to bind her to him. To bring space into the relationship, you must have the confidence to allow a woman to pull away from you and come back to you in her own time.

Many couples try to spend as much time as possible in each other's presence, especially when passions run high. You must learn to appreciate the speed with which a woman falls in love. A study published in the *Journal of Social Psychology* revealed that men fall in love faster than women and they also want intimacy a lot faster too.[106] Men and women frequently destroy the element of space by making themselves too available—they talk about everything, they see too much of each other, and they spend too much time together. This lack of space often leads to a severe drop in attraction. To overcome this problem, you must actively enforce the element of space, even if the thought of bringing space into the relationship makes you feel uncomfortable.

CASE STUDY #31: SUFFOCATING ATTRACTION

Jacob and Emily had been married for seven years when Emily dropped an unexpected bombshell: "I want a divorce," she told Jacob without a shred of emotion.

Jacob was shocked. What about the kids? How would this affect them, and why… why did she want a divorce when their life was so comfortable? Jacob knew their relationship had problems but was it so bad that they had to get divorced? The truth was, what had started out as an intimate and loving relationship had quickly disintegrated into a sexless marriage devoid of passion and intimacy. Despite this, Jacob still thought their marriage was worth saving. Emily, however, wasn't convinced. She wanted more, she wanted love, she wanted passion, and she wanted to feel alive. As far as Emily was concerned, her relationship with Jacob was dull and lifeless. Their days had become routine and predictable. After work, Jacob and Emily would come home and watch TV together. They would talk about their day and hold each other close. At night, as they got ready for bed, they would often shower together and brush their teeth at the same time. In fact, they were so comfortable being around each other, they often left the bathroom door open when they went to the toilet.

Now, when Emily looked at Jacob, it was like she was looking at a close friend. She no longer wanted to have sex with him, and she no longer thought about him or wondered what he was doing during the day. Emily remembered how, almost a year ago, she had tried bringing the element of space into their relationship. Emily knew she needed time to herself— time to think about their relationship and their future together. But every time she asked for space, Jacob would get upset and complain that she didn't love him. Emily felt trapped and suffocated. She now knew, without a shred of doubt, that she had no choice but to leave Jacob and never look back.

⅄

The moment you become predictable (either in thought or deed), is the moment you become boring, tiresome, unexciting, and unattractive. An attractive man doesn't make his romantic partner his primary concern. He doesn't need to be with her twenty-four hours a day, seven days a week. When you live a full and active life, the element of space will naturally be present in your relationships.

When a man and woman live together in a long-term relationship, it's still possible to introduce space by living a life that's separate from your partner. Whether this means working out separately, meeting your own friends, seeing family, or working on your own hobbies and projects, you must take the time to focus on yourself as opposed to cruising by in a co-dependent relationship. If you find it difficult to avoid being in the presence of your partner (for instance, if you're married with children), occasionally sleeping in separate beds is a great way to restore attraction and a dying sex life. The idea of sleeping in separate beds often induces a sense of panic among couples, as though their partner has somehow lost interest in them and is about to exit the relationship. Research, however, shows that sleeping in separate beds when in long-term relationships often helps to bring the element of space and attraction back into the relationship.[104] Many of the most successful long-term relationships, where both partners have a sustained, long-lasting desire for each other has come as a direct result of space being introduced through separate sleeping arrangements.

For the insecure and possessive man, the thought of giving a woman space is enough to send him into a downward spiral of frustration and anxiety. A relationship, however, should never feel like an obligation. There's nothing more unattractive than someone who forces their presence onto another person when that person has already expressed their desire for space. If attraction is to exist, the element of space must be present regardless of whether you feel comfortable with it or not.

NEVER USE LOGIC TO FIGHT EMOTION

Logic will never change emotion or perception.

— Edward de Bono

Women are predisposed to worry and anxiety. If you allow a woman's emotions to take over during the course of the relationship, her feelings of worry and anxiety will overwhelm her and consume you in the process. If a woman becomes moody or distant, there's a good chance she's allowed herself to become a victim of her own emotions. If you try to talk a woman out of her emotions using logic and reason, you'll have more success talking to a brick wall.

Reason and logic can never defeat emotion because emotion is neither logical nor reasonable. The more you attempt to reason with a woman, the more she'll resist. If a woman's acting distant towards you, it will be impossible to try and talk her into feeling warmth and affection using logic and reason. A woman doesn't care if she's right or wrong, she only cares about how she feels in the present. If she's feeling angry or sad, you won't be able to talk her into a state of happiness and bliss. Instead, you must allow her to talk and make it a point not to fix her problems.

CASE STUDY #32: THE SILENCE IS DEAFENING

Dylan and Abi were having lunch when Dylan noticed that Abi was unusually silent. Whenever Dylan tried to say something, Abi just gave him a weak smile and continued to play around with her food. Dylan was confused. One minute they were having a great time, fooling around in the kitchen; the next minute Abi was acting like Dylan had just killed the family dog.

"Did I do something wrong?" Dylan asked. Abi gave him a withering look.

"Why don't you just tell me if something's wrong?"

"I don't want to talk about it," Abi said.

"Talk about what?"

"I'm fine. Don't worry."

"Of course, I'm worried. You're obviously upset about something otherwise you wouldn't be acting this way."

Abi sneered and looked out the window.

"Please just tell me what's wrong. I hate to see you like this."

"See me like what?"

"Like you are now. Sad. Unhappy." Dylan took hold of Abi's hand. "Please don't shut me out. Has something happened at work? I know you're stressed out, but…" Abi pulled her hand away. "You're not even going to tell me what's wrong?" Dylan said. "Isn't that what people do when they love each other?"

"God, you're so annoying," Abi said as she got up from the table.

"Where are you going?"

"Away from you." And with that, Abi left the house, slamming the door behind her.

⅄

The moment a woman gets upset or pulls away, a flurry of thoughts rush through the man's head. His analytical brain goes into overdrive, asking the same question over and over: how can I fix the situation and make this woman happy? The short answer is *you can't fix her* and *you can't make her happy*. You should expect a woman's mood to fluctuate. You should expect her to be happy one minute and sad the next. And you should expect her to occasionally pull away from you. Fortunately, there are two simple ways to deal with this kind of behavior. The first is to remain indifferent to a woman's emotions no matter her emotional state; the second is to mirror her emotions and diffuse her negative energy.

MIRROR HER EMOTIONS

Sex relieves tension—love causes it.

— Woody Allen

Any man who's been in a serious relationship knows that women frequently pull away and create problems for no reason. When this happens, the man's natural instinct is to wonder why his girlfriend or wife is acting this way.

Sometimes there are legitimate reasons for a woman's behavior; at other times, there's no logical explanation except for a female predisposition towards emotional instability. Perhaps you've done something to upset her; perhaps she woke up on the wrong side of the bed, or perhaps she's testing you to see how you'll respond. Whatever the reason might be, the most important thing a woman wants to know is this: are you strong enough to handle her emotions or not?

CASE STUDY #33: FIGHT FIRE WITH FIRE

When Neil met Gretchen outside her apartment, he could tell straight away that she was in a bad mood. As usual, whenever Gretchen was upset her face was the picture of misery.

"Are you okay?" Neil asked as he came up beside her.

"I'm fine," Gretchen replied.

"Would you like to go for a walk?"

"Sure," Gretchen said. As they walked to the park, Gretchen told Neil how she had done yoga a couple of days ago and would try pilates next week.

"That's awesome," Neil said. "You're putting me to shame, you're so healthy."

"Why do you keep talking about my health?"

Neil looked confused. "I'm not."

"You asked me how I'm feeling, now you're telling me I'm healthy."

"I only asked because you told me you weren't feeling well the other day."

"Don't talk about my health," Gretchen snapped.

Neil had seen Gretchen act this way before and he knew it didn't bode well for the rest of the day. The last time Gretchen had acted this way, she had spent the whole day chewing him out. Neil didn't want to experience a repeat of that all over again, so Neil did what he thought was best and told Gretchen he "didn't mean anything by it, it was just a harmless comment." Neil then proceeded to spend the next couple of hours trying to talk Gretchen into a state of happiness, but nothing he said or did seemed to lighten her mood or make her feel any better.

* * *

Six months later, Neil was gone and Gretchen was in a relationship with Sean.

One afternoon, while Gretchen and Sean were having coffee, Sean asked Gretchen if she was feeling better. Gretchen had been sick for a couple of days and Sean wanted to make sure she was okay.

"I'm fine," Gretchen said, sipping her coffee.

"You sure?"

"I said I'm fine," Gretchen snapped.

"Relax, I was just making sure you're okay."

"Well, don't, it makes you sound stupid."

Fortunately, Sean had seen this kind of behavior before. He got up from the table and flashed Gretchen a smile. "You'll get the check, right?" And with that, he was gone. Sean knew there was nothing he could say to make Gretchen happy. And he knew she would spend the next couple of hours being rude and there was nothing he could do about it except mirror her emotions and withdraw from the situation. Actions, after all, speak louder than words.

As Sean walked out of the diner, Gretchen got up and followed him out the door. "Where are you going?" she yelled.

"I've got stuff to do."

"Are you mad at me? I didn't do anything."

"See ya," Sean said as he crossed the street. The way Sean saw it he was a busy guy. He had his own business, he loved to workout, and he had options with women. He didn't have time to waste on women who were rude and disrespectful.

* * *

Gretchen didn't contact Sean for the rest of the day, and Sean didn't contact her either. It was a classic standoff. Gretchen, however, was bristling with anxiety. Will I ever see him again? Is this it? What was I thinking? Why did I have to get so upset over nothing? she thought.

Later that night, Gretchen checked her phone… still no message from Sean. Unable to contain her anxiety any longer, Gretchen typed out a message and sent it to Sean: *"Hey, I'm sorry about before. Are you okay?"*

∧

If a woman's acting moody or withdrawn, all the talking in the world won't bring her back to a place of joy and happiness. Expressions of frustration and anger will only pour fuel on the situation as the woman comes to realize that she now has power over you and your emotions. In this situation, any attempt to placate a woman and soothe her will be met with sharp resistance. Instead, it's always better to mirror a woman's emotions to neutralize her power. When a woman pulls away from you, you must also pull away; when she grows distant and withdrawn, you too must become distant and withdrawn; and when she pushes you away by acting rude and disrespectful, simply withdraw your attention and refuse to empower her.

Imagine for a moment that a piece of string binds you to the woman you desire. Every time the string pulls tight, there's sexual tension in the relationship. Similarly, when the string goes slack, tension dies and attraction fades. When attraction fades and there's a loss of sexual interest, either you or the woman— preferably both—must pull away from each other to bring sexual tension back into the relationship.

When a woman pulls away or becomes emotionally distant, most men, in a desperate attempt to soothe their anxiety, try to close the distance, thus making the string go slack, killing all sexual tension and attraction in the process. Instead, when a woman pulls away, you must mirror her behavior and also pull away in response. This, once more, pulls the string tight, bringing sexual tension back into the relationship with force and vigor.

WOMEN ALWAYS TEST

Fire is the test of gold; adversity, of strong men.

— Martha Graham

Every man who's ever interacted with a woman has, at some point in time, been tested. Most men, however, go through life unaware that women test men on a daily basis. It's for this reason that so many men fail when it comes to seduction. Before we explore the different ways that women test men, it's important to understand why women test in the first place. At its core, a test is an easy way for a woman to determine whether a man is weak or strong.

Testing is not something that women consciously do, but something they've been programmed to do since birth. In the same way that babies are imprinted with a fear of snakes, women are imprinted with a need to test.[107] This stems from evolution and a woman's biological need to reproduce with the strongest DNA possible. A test is nature's way of helping a woman find the best genes for her future offspring. If you pass a woman's tests, she's more likely to believe you can father strong, healthy children. The reason why women test comes down to simple biology, but as you're about to discover, the way women test is anything but simple.

CASE STUDY #34: EVERYTHING'S A TEST

Jason and Amy were celebrating their one-year anniversary at Amy's favorite seafood restaurant. This was Jason's way of showing Amy how much he cared about her. After they finished dessert, the waiter brought some cocktails over to the table—a piña colada for Jason and a daiquiri for Amy.

"Wow," Jason exclaimed. "They look good."

Amy raised the daiquiri to her lips and took a sip. "Ughhh," she groaned.

"No good?"

"That's disgusting."

"Want to try mine?"

Amy grabbed Jason's piña colada and took a sip. "Oh, that's much better. I'm keeping this one," Amy said.

"Let me try the daiquiri." Jason lifted the daiquiri to his lips and took a sip. She was right, it tasted terrible—too much alcohol and way too sour. Jason pushed the daiquiri to one side and turned his attention back to Amy.

An hour later, Jason and Amy were getting ready to leave when Amy saw the daiquiri resting on the table.

"You're not going to drink it?" Amy asked.

"Nah, you're right, it's way too sour."

"Oh, go on," Amy goaded. "I dare you."

"No way!" Jason laughed. "I'm not drinking that."

Amy looked at Jason, then, with a cheeky smile, leaned in and whispered, "If you drink it, I'll give you the most amazing night of sex you've ever had."

"You serious?"

"Of course."

"You've got yourself a deal." And with that, Jason picked up the daiquiri and swallowed it down in one gulp.

* * *

Later that night, Amy was curled up in bed at Jason's apartment when she heard Jason step out of the shower and walk into the bedroom. Jason approached the bed and kissed Amy on the cheek, letting his towel drop to the floor.

Jason couldn't wait to get into bed and claim his reward. In the shower, Jason had wondered what Amy meant when she said: "...the most amazing night of sex you've ever had." What exactly was she going to do to him? Jason could barely contain his excitement as he pulled back the covers and climbed into bed. Jason placed his hand on Amy's stomach. "You're so soft and warm."

"I'm so drunk," Amy responded.

"You only had one drink."

Amy stiffened and rolled over onto her stomach. Jason lifted himself up and kissed her on the cheek.

"Uhhh," Amy moaned. "I'm kind of tired."

"I thought we were going to make love?" Jason said, a touch of frustration creeping into his voice.

"I'm tired!"

"Come on," Jason said. "A deal's a deal. You made me drink that disgusting cocktail, right?"

"I didn't make you drink anything."

"I only drank it because we made a deal," Jason said, trying his best to stay calm.

Amy pulled the covers over her face. "I can't remember, I'm drunk."

"You said we'd have the most amazing sex if I drank it."

"Well, now we can't can we? You've totally ruined the moment."

Jason was hit with the sudden realization that Amy was just kidding around. A sense of relief washed over him as he bent down and kissed her on the lips.

"I told you, I'm tired!" Amy snapped.

"What do you mean tired?" Amy didn't respond. "Are you serious?" Jason said. "You promised we'd have sex, now you're backing out. I can't believe this."

* * *

The next morning, when Jason woke up, Amy was already dressed.

"You're leaving?" Jason said, still groggy with sleep.

Amy came over to the bed and kissed him on the cheek. "I've got to run some errands, then have lunch with my sister. How do I look?" Amy said, spinning around in a bright blue dress.

"You look great," Jason muttered. "You're leaving so early?"

"Sorry, honey. I'll call you tonight." Amy smiled as she walked out the door.

* * *

Later that night, Jason paced around his apartment, waiting for Amy's call. It was almost 10 p.m. and he was starting to get worried. Jason picked up his phone and sent Amy a message: *"Hey, how was lunch with sis?"*

An hour went by… still no response. It was now 11 p.m. That's strange, Jason thought. Maybe something's happened. I better call and make sure she's okay. Amy's phone rang and rang... still no response. Something wasn't right. First, she refused to have sex with him and now she wasn't answering her phone. Jason began to sense that Amy was either pulling away from him or about to leave him. Then another even more devastating thought struck him— maybe she's met someone else. Jason tried calling again... still no answer. In a fit of rage, Jason threw his phone across the room and kicked a cushion lying on the floor.

The next morning, Jason continued to send Amy a stream of messages, trying to find out where she was, and, more importantly, find out why she had pulled away from him. Unbeknown to Jason was the fact that Amy would never have sex with him again, and she would only see him a couple more times after that. He had failed all her tests and Amy's attraction for him was now at an all-time low.

ᐱ

When a woman withdraws from the relationship, it's crucial to see her behavior for what it is—a test. The moment you sense a woman pull away (either by appearing disinterested or refusing to answer your messages or return your phone calls) you should assume that she's testing you. When this happens, you mustn't let insecurity and panic get the better of you; instead, you must display strength and indifference in response to her behavior. All it takes is a willingness to step outside your comfort zone and embrace uncertainty. A woman might not get in touch with you for a couple of days, she might not get in touch for a week, regardless how long it takes her to get back to you, you must have the strength of character to walk away until she contacts you.

THE BITCH TEST

When a woman intentionally acts rude, bitchy, or disrespectful, she's trying to get a measure of your strength using what's commonly known as the *bitch test*. In this situation, a woman might question your masculinity and attack you in ways she knows will get under your skin. She might try to provoke you and use any method she can to rattle you. She might make an off-handed comment about your lack of physical strength (if you're skinny); or if you're short, she might make a disparaging comment about your height. These comments are designed to expose your weakness and find out whether or not you're confident or insecure. When this happens, there's no point getting into a heated discussion, trying to defend yourself with logic and reason—if you do, you fail her test. Women are skilled at uncovering weakness, and once a woman finds a chink in your armor, she won't curtail her attack until you shore up your defenses.

A lot of men assume a "tough guy" persona only to fall apart the moment a woman tests them. Even the most masculine men who are, for all intents and purposes, alpha, still find themselves emotionally vulnerable to a woman's unexpected psychological attack. In the face of rude and disrespectful behavior, it's important to handle the situation the right way. Instead of giving in to temptation and exploding in a fit of rage, it's always better to keep a cool head and walk away.

THE JEALOUSY TEST

Women often use jealousy as a way to expose weakness and test men. The woman starts off, innocently enough, by talking about another man who may or may not have shown interest in her. The instinct to *mate guard* immediately triggers strong feelings of jealousy. It is, therefore, no surprise that jealousy is one of the easiest emotions to exploit. Once a woman sets her jealousy trap, she's looking for one thing and one thing only: your reaction to the situation. If you get jealous and feel threatened by another man, the woman will start to question you and wonder why you're acting so insecure.

A woman's jealousy test should always be handled with indifference or humor to shrink the situation down into an issue of minor importance. This proves that you're not the least bit concerned or threatened by the presence of another man. The man who comes from a place of strength knows his true value, and he knows that if a woman cheats on him, he can easily find another woman to replace her. If you fly into a jealous rage, get upset, or become passive aggressive, the woman will attribute your behavior to insecurity—insecurity that translates into weakness. Is it because you feel like you can't compete or because you feel like you're not good enough? Love rivals will always be present as long as humans exist. The attractive man doesn't concern himself with potential love rivals unless they stray too far into his domain.

HOW TO PASS EVERY TEST

When you meet a woman for the first time, the woman doesn't know if you're strong or weak, stable or unstable, secure or insecure. And even though she might enjoy your company and find you physically attractive, a woman won't have a measure of your true strength until she's tested you. Every time you pass a woman's test, you move one step closer to proving your value. This is why you must never get frustrated when women test you. Instead, you must view a test as a healthy challenge that must be handled the right way.

If you eliminate weak responses from your repertoire, you'll find it that much easier to pass a woman's tests whenever you encounter them. To make it easier to deal with women in times of conflict, it's always useful to ask yourself one important question: am I acting in a way that's insecure, or am I acting in a way that's confident? Any actions that come from a place of fear and insecurity must be eliminated and replaced with actions based on strength and confidence. To project strength and confidence, it's useful to keep the following guidelines in mind:

— Don't try to control her
— Never beg, plead, or cry
— Never ask for forgiveness
— Never become aggressive
— Avoid showing signs of jealousy
— Never make a woman your top priority
— Don't try to reason, explain, and apologize

— Don't chase her with messages and phone calls
— If she withdraws her attention, never chase her
— Remain indifferent to her emotions and moods
— Take the focus off the woman and focus on yourself instead
— Deflect rude, disrespectful behavior with humor and indifference

One question that often comes up is whether women consciously test men or not? The answer is both *yes* and *no*. A woman is always testing you, and she's always looking to get a measure of your strength to see how you handle yourself in difficult situations. If you react with weakness and insecurity, a woman will pull away from you and continue to test you until she either loses all attraction for you or you shore up your weakness and she comes to realize that you're high-value and it's safe for her to continue to invest her emotions into you.

INDUCE SCARCITY TO INCREASE YOUR VALUE

*If you tell me I can't have something then
that just makes me want it more.*

— Anna Benson

One of the least understood and unappreciated aspects of seduction is the concept of value. Between a man that's available and a man that's less available, who do you think is more attractive to women? In a study published in the *Journal of Personality and Social Psychology* researchers examined how people would react to two identical sets of cookies placed in separate glass jars.[108] One jar contained ten cookies, and the other jar contained two cookies. The researchers then attempted to find out which jar of cookies would be perceived as more valuable (even though the cookies and jars were both identical). The results of the study found that the jar with two cookies was rated more valuable than the jar with ten cookies. It's a strange quirk of human nature that less available people and objects are perceived to be more desirable and valuable.

When gold is as common as dirt, it has no value. Water is arguably the most important element on earth. It sustains life and keeps us alive. As humans, we can only survive for approximately three to four days without water. Despite water's obvious value, however, water is still considered a low-value commodity because its supply is abundant. Yet, gold an element that does nothing to support life is considered more valuable than water because its supply is limited.

This brings us to an interesting point, out of all the human emotions, human beings are most uncomfortable dealing with feelings of loss, regret, and missed opportunity. Losing out on a scarce resource has the potential to trigger a cocktail of negative emotions, and, as research into *loss aversion* shows people are much more likely to want to avoid loss than they are to seek gains.[109] In other words, the pain of losing fifty dollars far outweighs the joy of winning fifty dollars. Once you have a firm understanding of these concepts, you can start to use scarcity and loss aversion to your advantage, exploiting a woman's natural instinct to mate and pair with high-value men.

CASE STUDY #35: LOW VALUE = LOW ATTRACTION

Zach and Brooke had been dating for almost two years when Zach got down on one knee and asked Brooke to marry him. Zach knew he wasn't going to find anyone better than Brooke, even if he spent the next ten years looking. Now in his mid-forties, Zach couldn't wait to settle down and start a family. Sure, their relationship wasn't perfect and they sometimes fought, but who didn't? The more he thought about it, the more Zach knew he wanted to spend the rest of his life with Brooke.

Logically, Brooke knew marrying Zach made sense. After all, he was a loyal and loving boyfriend and would make an equally devoted husband. Zach was Mr. Reliable, and Brooke loved that about him. Yet for some reason, she couldn't help but feel like something was missing from their relationship. It wasn't that Zach wasn't a good man, he was. But where was all the passion and excitement she craved? If Brooke was being honest with herself, she knew she was just passing time, waiting for Mr. Right to come along. This can't go on, Brooke thought. It's not fair to Zach and it's not fair to me.

* * *

Nine months later, Brooke was in a relationship with Daniel. Daniel was the complete opposite of Zach. He was exciting, interesting, and bold. The sex was incredible, the conversation was interesting, and they had enough passion and excitement in their relationship to last a lifetime. There was only one problem—Brooke felt as though she liked Daniel a lot more than he liked her. She also felt as though she had to work overtime to get his attention. She was the one who was always calling him and sending him messages. Daniel's elusive presence had turned him into a scarce resource. Little did Brooke realize that this was the main reason why she was so attracted to him.

⅄

Basic human psychology dictates that men who are less available are seen as more valuable and attractive than their more available peers. Research into attraction has also confirmed that playing "hard to get" works in a man's favor.[110] This is why being a scarce resource is such a powerful and effective way to gain a woman's respect and raise your own value at the same time. However, being a scarce resource isn't just a matter of pulling away and becoming less available, it's about becoming less emotionally available to induce confusion and turmoil.

Emotional withdrawal means you disqualify a woman when she (a) attempts to get close to you or (b) pulls away from you. As an example, when a woman tries to draw close to you by saying: "So what are we?" It's easy to disqualify her with a simple: "I'm not looking for anything serious right now." This statement is loaded with subtext, providing hope and doubt in equal measure. "I'm not looking for anything serious" sets up the challenge, "...right now" offers a glimmer of hope and something for her to work towards. In the same way, if a woman tries to pull away from you by telling you that "things are moving too fast," you must agree with this sentiment and let her know you feel the same way and miss your freedom. Pushing a woman away when she pulls away from you increases your value, forcing her to chase you as she tries to capture that one elusive commodity more valuable than gold—your love. If you seek love, you must act as though love is the last thing on your mind. In the same way, if you seek commitment, you must make freedom your number one priority.

STAY OUT OF THE FRIEND ZONE

She had a place in his life, he never made her think twice.

— "What a Fool Believes," The Doobie Brothers

If you want to become intimate with a woman, you must avoid the friend zone at all costs. The moment you become friends with a woman instead of becoming intimate with her is the moment you sacrifice seduction in favor of friendship. A study run by the University of Wisconsin explained how men have a hard time being just friends and often want more.[111] The Wisconsin study also discovered that men and women mostly have no idea how other people feel about them, as in: does this person find me attractive? Men, however, are more likely to assume a woman is romantically interested in them, while women are more likely to assume that men have no romantic interest in them at all. Complicating the issue further, a lot of men willingly enter the friend zone because they fear rejection and have low self-confidence. These same men believe that if they become friends with a woman first, they'll be able to turn her into their girlfriend later on.

CASE STUDY #36: FRIENDS FOREVER

Ethan was attracted to Juliana the moment he saw her sitting outside the college library. If only I could be with a girl like that, Ethan thought. She's perfect.

A couple of weeks later, a mutual friend introduced Ethan to Juliana. From that moment on, Ethan decided he would make it his mission to get to know Juliana. He would become her friend first, then turn her into his girlfriend later on once they got to know each other.

The more Juliana got to know Ethan, the more she liked him. He was cute and easy to talk to. He would often spend hours listening to her talk about all her problems, and he never tried to control her or tell her what to do. Of course Juliana knew that Ethan liked her, but how could she take him seriously? He reminded her of a big, cute puppy dog. If she was being truly honest with herself, there was a moment when Juliana thought Ethan was kind of attractive, but he never made a move and always seemed so shy and timid around her.

* * *

A couple of months later, Juliana was at the gym when she met Ed. Ed wasn't the kind of guy to waste time and he let Juliana know straight away that he found her attractive. Juliana was instantly smitten by Ed's confidence and charm. She was so excited she couldn't wait to get back to her dorm and tell all her friends about him.

That evening, Juliana couldn't stop talking about Ed and how she thought he was so charming and handsome. Juliana's friend were all excited to hear the news—everyone, that is, except for Ethan.

Later that night, as Ethan and Juliana walked through the college campus, Ethan knew he had to confront Juliana about her new love interest. "You can't trust strangers," Ethan said. "Guys like Ed don't respect women and they're only after one thing."

Juliana smiled. "You don't have to worry about me."

Ethan felt a surge of panic. He knew he had to make a move now or risk losing Juliana forever. "Juliana, there's something I need to tell you. This might sound strange, but I really like you."

Juliana took a moment to compose herself. "Oh, Ethan, that's sweet of you... but honestly, you're such a great friend. I don't want to lose you."

"You wouldn't lose me," Ethan replied.

"I would. It wouldn't be the same."

"I'm sorry," Ethan choked. "I shouldn't have said anything."

"No, it's sweet of you. You're one of my best friends Ethan. We're great like we are, can't you see that?"

"I can, I know. I don't know what I was thinking." Ethan replied.

"You're so cute," Juliana said, "Have you been drinking?"

"Maybe just a little."

"Ha, I knew it. You're hilarious. See you tomorrow." And with that Juliana smiled and waved goodbye, leaving Ethan standing alone on the sidewalk.

⋏

When you let a woman put you in the friend zone, you're subconsciously telling her that you don't have the confidence to seduce her. Consider the implications of a study carried out by researchers at the University of Virginia and Pennsylvania State University where researchers observed that less than 10 percent of couples started out as just friends.[112] Not great odds if you're looking to turn that attractive "girl friend" into a "girlfriend." A woman knows when a man wants to be more than just friends. At the same time, a woman also knows when a man is too weak to make a move and seduce her. This is the reason why so many men are condemned to the friend zone. There's nothing more unattractive and unappealing to women than a man who's too afraid to express himself and seduce a woman he finds attractive.

Early in the seduction process, there's a good chance a woman will, at some point, try to friend zone you. Often, this is just a test to see if you're prepared to accept a weakened position or do you have the guts to seduce her? The weak man fails the test every time, while the attractive man rejects the woman's offer and lets her know that friendship is off the table. If a woman says: "We should just be friends." You must respond with a simple: "Sorry, not interested." This response immediately disqualifies the woman and lets her know that friendship is not an option. This form of disqualification works in much the same way that the *Romeo and Juliet effect* makes people more desirable (by making your love hard to acquire, you become more desirable and attractive in the same way that Romeo and Juliet's attraction for each other flourished the moment they were told they couldn't see each other). Even in long-term relationships, after years of marriage, a woman might still try to put you in the friend zone. It's up to you to decide whether or not you're willing to accept her offer of friendship or hold out for intimacy.

SHE MUST INVEST IN YOU

Commitment is an act, not a word.

— Jean-Paul Sartre

Most men believe that if they buy a woman gifts, take her out for dinner, and show her love and affection, they will, according to logic, receive the same amount of love and affection in return.[113] The attractive man, however, understands that his investment in a woman is nowhere near as important as her investment in him. If we consider all the various forms of investment that exist within a relationship, the main forms of investment are: (1) emotional: investing one's emotions and feelings into someone; (2) time: spent thinking about someone, or time spent with them; (3) physical: sharing physical intimacy with another person; and (4) financial: buying gifts or spending money on someone. All of these forms of investment lead to higher levels of commitment and attraction on the part of the investor.

The man who invests all his time, money, effort, and emotions into one woman values that woman a lot more than the man who makes no investment whatsoever. If you invest in someone, you are much more likely to value that person.[114] Whether your investment is good or bad is beside the point, the feeling of value remains, making it increasingly difficult with each additional level of investment to withdraw your emotions and walk away if the investment turns out to be bad. This is the danger of the *sunk cost fallacy*, which states that the more you invest in someone or something, the harder it becomes to walk away, even if that investment turns out to be a bad decision. It's for this reason alone that people find it so hard to exit a relationship, even when the relationship becomes toxic. The idea of leaving someone when so much has already been invested is often too much to bear. Understanding how investment works in relationships will not only protect you from future loss it will also help you build greater levels of attraction.

In pure Machiavellian style, the man who's selfish encourages women to invest in him for he understands one simple truth: the more a woman invests in him, the more committed she'll be. If your goal is to ensnare a woman, you must be selfish, you must be ruthless, and you must be willing to take more than you give. Some dark research into attraction shows that women who invest in men by taking risks (as in having unprotected sex) are more likely to value the relationship than if they had taken no risks at all.[115] The charming yet ever selfish rogue builds attraction by getting women to invest in him. He knows only too well that every additional act of devotion and investment brings the woman further under his spell.

CASE STUDY #37: THE ATTRACTIVE BAD GUY

Joel was lost for words. His dream girl, Jocelyn, had spent the last two hours talking about Cole—that selfish asshole who treated her like shit. Joel struggled to keep his cool as Jocelyn told him what a terrible guy Cole was. The list of charges against Cole was both long and depressing: (1) forgetting Jocelyn's birthday; (2) taking gifts from Jocelyn and never buying anything in return; (3) having sex with Jocelyn while making no attempt to get her off; (4) refusing to spend the weekend with Jocelyn; (5) hanging out with his friends instead of hanging out with Jocelyn. And that was just scratching the surface. It was enough to make Joel's blood boil.

What was even worse was the fact that Cole refused to commit to Jocelyn and be her "official boyfriend." What the hell's wrong with him? Joel thought. I'm here. I'm ready to commit. Why can't she see that? Joel was even more frustrated by the fact that two years ago he was the one sitting where Cole is now. What the hell happened? He had been nothing but kind, loving, and supportive in their relationship. He remembered Jocelyn's birthday; he remembered their anniversary; he always bought her gifts and showered her with love and attention; he must have given her over a hundred massages; not to mention all the effort he made trying to please her in bed. And for what? Jocelyn had never rewarded him for being a good boyfriend. Instead, she had punished him by insisting they were better off as friends.

Now, here she was torturing him in the worst possible way. And Joel couldn't believe what he was hearing. The woman he loved was telling him that even though Cole was the most selfish, arrogant son of a bitch she had ever met, she still loved him. Cole, she said, was her "one true love." And one day he would love her as much as she loved him. Joel had to bite his tongue to stop himself from screaming.

⋏

Look around and you'll see countless examples of men over-investing in women every day. There's the man who buys gifts; there's the man who cooks for hours; there's the man who spends lavishly; there's the man who gives massages; and there's the man who tries to please women any way he can. Consider the following question: could you imagine someone you admire, a truly powerful and attractive man doing any of the above to try and seduce a woman?

Once you pull back the curtain to reveal the inner-workings of the female mind, a plain and simple truth is revealed: women only value that which they work for. If your love is easy to acquire, a woman will naturally find it that much harder to respect you and appreciate you. Conversely, if a woman has to work hard for your attention, pouring all her emotions, time, and energy into you in an effort to win you over, you become infinitely more valuable and attractive.

DEALING WITH CONFLICT

*The supreme art of war is to subdue
the enemy without fighting.*

— Sun Tzu

In any relationship, the question: how can I handle
difficult situations the right way often enters a man's
mind after he finds himself, once more, dealing with
unexpected conflict. When women bring turmoil into
your life, it's important to know how to handle the
situation the right way. If you stumble your way
through emotionally charged situations, you'll not
only come across as weak and unattractive you'll end
up feeling frustrated and resentful towards the woman
in your life as she becomes increasingly difficult to
appease.

CASE STUDY #38: NEUTRALIZE NEGATIVE ENERGY

Steve and Isabel had been living together for two
months when Isabel discovered a text message on
Steve's phone. The message was from Steve's ex-
girlfriend.

"You forgot your phone!" Isabel screamed the
moment Steve came home.

"What's wrong?" Steve replied.

"Who's Candice?" Isabel threw Steve's phone
across the room.

"What are you talking about? Candice my ex?" Steve set his bag down on the table. "It's probably an old message or something."

"Bullshit," Isabel fumed. "You're lying. You're just trying to cover up the fact you still have feelings for her."

"Where do you think I was just now, with Candice?"

"You could be."

"Yeah," Steve smiled. "I could be. I gotta get something to eat, you hungry?" Steve walked into the kitchen.

Isabel watched him closely. He doesn't even care. How can he be so calm about everything? "You're an asshole," she shouted after him.

Steve rummaged through the fridge, looking for something to eat. "We don't have any food. You want to go out or get takeaway?"

"I'll take care of it," Isabel said, getting up from the couch. She stepped into the kitchen and wrapped her arms around Steve, squeezing him from behind. "I'm sorry, I just get so jealous sometimes. Forgive me?"

"Only if you buy me dinner," Steve replied.

When a woman levels accusations at you, whether those accusations are true or not, your best form of defense is to agree and amplify. She threatens to leave, your response should be, "Great, no more headaches." She calls you a liar, tell her you've been called worse. She calls you an asshole, tell her you'll take it as a compliment. You must show no sign of weakness—weakness that infects so many emotionally charged situations. You know better than to engage a woman head on and try to convince her through logic and reason that you're one of the good guys. Instead, you must do the unexpected and pivot. Agree with everything she says and even exaggerate her claims to the point where she questions her own sanity. Agree and amplify is a simple strategy that helps neutralize highly charged, emotional situations. This ensures you remain attractive, even when a woman attacks you.

HANDLING JEALOUSY

*Never underestimate the power of jealousy
and the power of envy to destroy.*

— Oliver Stone

Men and women all experience jealousy to some degree, we just experience jealousy in different ways. For example, women are more likely to feel jealous if their romantic partner falls in love with another woman; men, on the other hand, are more likely to feel jealous if their romantic partner has sex with another man. This is a key difference between the sexes. If you think your girlfriend or wife is interested in someone else, or another man has shown interest in your woman, it's natural to feel jealous. In psychology, this is known as *mate guarding*, which describes the defensive response that's triggered when facing sexual competition. It's normal to feel jealous. It's normal to mate guard. It's normal to want to protect your woman from other men. But knowing how to protect a woman the right way is what separates the attractive man from the unattractive man.

If you believe your girlfriend or wife has cheated on you or is about to cheat on you, those initial feelings of hurt, jealousy, and anger can be overwhelming. The natural response is to destroy the man that's sexually defiled your partner. Submitting to your emotions, however, will do nothing to fix the problem or make those feelings of jealousy go away. You must remember that jealousy is a temporary emotion. But because it's such a primal emotion, it's impossible to eliminate jealousy altogether. Eliminating jealousy, however, is an exercise in futility. Instead, it's better to know how to handle jealousy the right way so you don't kill attraction and turn a woman off.

CASE STUDY #39: JEALOUSY LOVES INSECURITY

Glen was celebrating Christmas with his girlfriend Hope at her family home in the Berkshires when he noticed that Hope was spending a lot of time messaging people on her phone. Who's she talking to? And dammit, how could she do this to me? I need to find out what's going on, Glen thought.

Later that evening, when Hope was in the shower, Glen crept into Hope's bedroom and checked her phone. On the screen, he saw a message from a guy called Kevin. Who the fuck is Kevin?

* * *

The following day, Glen was watching TV when he saw Hope message someone on her phone and smile. How could she be so disrespectful? Glen thought as he gripped the edge of the sofa. "Look, we need to talk," Glen said. "You can't be texting other guys when I'm here with you."

"What do you mean?" Hope said.

"You're supposed to be on holiday with me."

"I'm just talking to my friend."

"Bullshit you're talking to your friend."

"What are you talking about?" Hope said.

"You know what I'm talking about."

"Jeez, it's nothing. I'm not going to turn my phone off just because I'm with you," Hope snapped.

* * *

That night, Glen couldn't sleep. He tossed and turned and all he could think about was Hope texting Kevin and all the other men who obviously wanted to have sex with her. What's she texting them anyway? Are they having text sex? Are they sending dick pics? Is she actually having sex with them?

"Are you okay?" Hope reached out and touched Glen on the shoulder.

"I'm fine," Glen said as he lay awake, staring at the ceiling. "Actually, I'm not. I don't think you should be texting other guys when you're with me."

"Are you serious?"

"Who are you talking to anyway?"

"It's nothing, I told you."

"I don't believe you."

"Believe what you want," Hope said.

"Show me your phone."

"Good night," Hope said as she turned away from Glen, pulling the duvet cover away from him. Glen was half-right about one thing—Hope was talking to other men, but she had friend zoned them all a long time ago. In her mind, Hope was telling the truth when she told Glen it was nothing to worry about. At least it wasn't anything to worry about until Glen had decided to make a big deal out of it.

* * *

Two years later, Hope was sitting in a new apartment watching TV with Jack (her new boyfriend) when Hope pulled out her phone.

"A guy approached me today and asked for my number," Hope said.

"Awesome," Jack grunted.

"What?"

"Take it as a compliment. It means you're still hot."

Hope was caught by surprise. Glen had spent half his time worrying about other guys, and the rest of his time trying to check her phone. Why wasn't Jack acting the same way or getting upset?

"He was kind of cute too," Hope said.

"I bet he was."

"It doesn't bother you that a guy asked for my number?"

"Why would it bother me?" Jack said. "You're a woman, guys are gonna hit on you."

Hope didn't know what to say. Not only was Jack not jealous, but somehow he had managed to make her feel as though "being hit on" was an everyday occurrence that happened to all woman. Jack was the complete opposite of Glen. He didn't care if other guys talked to her, and he didn't show any sign of jealousy or insecurity. Hope put her phone down and snuggled up close to Jack, resting her head on his shoulder. Hope didn't know why, but it felt so good to be close to this man.

⋏

It's not uncommon for women to use men as proxy weapons against each other as a way of finding out if a man is confident or insecure. Your job, as always, is to project strength and confidence, even in the most challenging circumstances. It's tempting to explode with rage, to call a woman out, to become passive aggressive, and use every trick in the book to punish her for making you feel jealous. All of these reactions do nothing but reveal insecurity and emotional weakness.

The only time you should worry about a woman leaving you for another man is when you allow feelings of jealousy to consume you. If you respond to feelings of jealousy with threats, tears, or moody behavior, don't be surprised if the woman decides she doesn't want to stick around to see the show. It's better, instead, to handle jealousy with an attitude of indifference. Try to find humor in the situation. Humor tells women you're unafraid and unaffected by feelings of jealousy. And where the unattractive man lets feelings of jealousy consume him and destroy the relationship, the attractive man acts in a way that is counter-intuitive and surprising.

RESTORE DYING ATTRACTION

*The fear of loss is greater
than the desire for gain.*

— Zig Ziglar

When a woman has lost attraction for a man to the
point where she believes she has no choice but to end
the relationship, it's not enough to simply pull away to
restore attraction. A woman's emotions must be
spiked, and her cortisol levels lit ablaze if you're to
have any chance at keeping the relationship alive. In
other words, you must make a woman feel dread and
anxiety to capture her interest and reignite the passion
in your relationship. But why would you want to instill
dread and anxiety in a woman just to capture her
interest? After all, isn't a warm and loving relationship
all about fighting through the tough times and
showing a woman how much you care, even when she
pulls away from you and makes your life difficult?
Isn't it better to forgive and forget than to stir up
trouble?

The path to forgiveness is littered with the broken
bodies of countless men who once extolled the virtues
of love and kindness only to be left broken and
defeated on the scrapheap of rejection. When a
woman wants to end the relationship, all the love and
kindness in the world won't bring her back to you. In
this situation, you must use a more powerful strategy.

You must introduce dread and uncertainty into the relationship to rebuild value and restore interest.

Introducing dread and uncertainty into the relationship sends several signals to a woman all at once: first, you're telling the woman you're high value and you have options; second, you make her feel anxious, which captures her attention; third, you become a scarce resource and thus become more valuable; and fourth, the woman feels as though she's about to lose you forever. She thought she was the one with all the power, now she's forced to re-evaluate that assumption. Remember, the purpose of dread is to recalibrate a woman's emotions and rebuild attraction. Listed below are some of the most effective ways to rebuild attraction by introducing dread and uncertainty into the relationship.

— Tell her you miss being single and you're not sure if you want to be in a relationship. This sudden desire for freedom will trigger her fear of loss receptors, bringing her attention squarely back onto you.

— Openly and without shame look at other women in public and talk about how attractive they are.

— Ignore her phone calls and text messages for days on end, forcing her to come to you in a sweat-induced panic as she tries to find out what's going on.

— Post pictures of yourself on social media with other women around you.

— Text and call other women in front of her. You can also text other people while she's with you. When she asks who you're talking to, keep things vague by telling her to "relax, it's just a friend."

— Start exercising (if you don't already), buy new clothes, and wear nice fragrances. She'll notice these subtle changes and she'll start to wonder whether or not you're seeing other women.

— Go on dates with other women. If she finds out, shrug and tell her you thought she wouldn't mind given her current behavior.

— Tell her you're going to have sex with other women and that she doesn't need to bother you again with her lack of sex and shitty attitude. This will trigger intense feelings of jealousy in conjunction with the fear of losing you—a double dose of anxiety that's guaranteed to make her work that much harder to keep you.

— Lightly spray yourself with a woman's fragrance. When she asks why you smell of perfume, tell her you were sampling fragrances. It's no lie, you were. But she won't believe it for a second.

— Tell her you're going away on holiday and you're not sure if you'll be able to speak to her while you're away. She'll wonder where you're going and who you're going with. Again, it's better to keep things vague. Let anxiety and space work to your advantage.

A lot of men are terrified that if they implement these strategies they'll lose a woman forever. The reality is if you don't implement these strategies you will lose her forever, especially if your girlfriend or wife has already withdrawn from the relationship and no longer respects you. As a general rule, when employing these strategies, the less said the better. You must never apologize for your behavior or show any sign of weakness.

Studies show that women are more attracted to men who put them into a fearful and anxious state. Once more, anxiety proves to be a crucial component of attraction. One study published in the *Archives of Sexual Behavior* found that women are more likely to find men attractive after they've taken a ride on a roller coaster.[116] The study found that "residual arousal from riding the roller-coaster intensified the participants' later experience of attraction." In a follow-up study conducted by McKendree University, researchers discovered that feelings of physical arousal and attraction don't stem exclusively from fear and anxiety. The McKendree study noted that 15 minutes of exercise was enough to elevate a woman's adrenaline to the point where she was more likely to experience feelings of attraction for another person.[117]

CASE STUDY #40: ANXIETY BREEDS ATTRACTION

When Aiden got home he opened his laptop and checked his email—only on the screen it wasn't his inbox. The browser was logged in to his wife's email account. Aiden was about to sign out when he noticed an email addressed to his wife Maria. The email was from a man he had never heard of before, and the subject line read: *"RE: Can't stop thinking about you."* Suspicious, Aiden opened the email, then spent the next hour trawling through Maria's inbox. It wasn't long before Aiden discovered that his wife of two years was having an emotional affair with a colleague at work. From what Aiden could see, Maria was the one chasing the guy. Her co-worker didn't even seem to be that interested or responsive. He was just being polite by responding to her emails. Now it all made perfect sense—the lack of sex, the cold, disrespectful behavior. Aiden finally understood why his wife was pulling away from him and didn't want to be around him anymore.

Later that day, when Maria came home from work, Aiden decided to confront her and find out what was going on. Maria didn't deny the charges against her. She told Aiden she still loved him but she was no longer attracted to him. This was the reason, she said, why she no longer wanted to have sex with him and why she had considered having an affair with her colleague (if only her colleague had been interested).

Aiden was devastated. He buried his head in his hands and sobbed. Maria sat on the couch, cold and emotionless. She was surprised to discover that she felt nothing. No emotion or pity. If anything, she was relieved. Relieved she no longer had to pretend she cared about the relationship. Relieved she no longer had to make excuses not to have sex.

As Aiden continued to sob, Maria took a moment to think about Matt—the only man she had ever truly loved. What happened to Matt and why did he leave her? Maria had conveniently forgotten that she had once treated Matt the same way she was now treating Aiden. She had flirted with other guys and she was often cold and dismissive, only Matt was different to Aiden. At the first sign of trouble, Matt told Maria he was happy she was flirting with other guys because he loved talking to other women too. Maybe they could even have an open relationship. Maria didn't like the sound of that. She tried throwing a tantrum and even threatened to leave, but Matt simply responded by disappearing from her life. When Matt finally resurfaced a couple of weeks later, he didn't even apologize. From that point on, Maria decided she would make it her mission to win Matt over. She would pour all her energy into him and make him fall in love with her. Unfortunately, things hadn't worked out the way she had planned.

Now, as Maria sat in the living room with Aiden weeping in front of her, all she could think about was Matt. Where was he and what was he doing? Would he still remember her? Maria wondered if she still had Matt's number lying around somewhere.

᛬

Research published in the *Journal of Personality and Social Psychology* found evidence for heightened levels of sexual attraction in conditions where high levels of anxiety exist.[118] In one example, the study found that men and women are likely to throw caution to the wind and indulge in extremely promiscuous behavior during times of war.[119] This desire for sexual intercourse arises, not from a state of safety and security, but from a state of fear and anxiety. Because the purpose of humanity is to reproduce, an imminent threat to life triggers extreme levels of sexual desire to ensure the survival of the species. It is, however, still easy to activate this fear/sex response in women by injecting uncertainty and anxiety into a dying relationship.

Part of the reason why so many people stay in toxic relationships stems from the fact that toxic relationships are the perfect breeding ground for anxiety. One unusual aspect of stress is that key stress hormones are also responsible for eliciting pleasure in the brain. As a result, women can become addicted "biochemically" to stressful, negative, or life-threatening situations when they become hooked on the chemical release that occurs during stressful situations. This is the primary reason why a woman can be so angry and upset with a man, yet find him so attractive at the same time.

Fear and dread are closely linked to human survival. Implementing dread game is a simple way to trick a woman's brain into thinking her survival is at stake. At a biological level, inducing dread activates a woman's fear receptors, releasing endorphins, cortisol, adrenaline, and norepinephrine into the woman's body, causing wave after wave of anxiety and sexual tension. This chemical release now brings the woman's focus onto the source of her anxiety—you. And just as she was about to forget you, you once more become the focus of her attention.

THE X FACTOR

*People may hear your words
but they feel your attitude.*

— Adam C. Maxwell

The idea that attraction flourishes in a swamp of anxiety, selfishness, and uncertainty doesn't sit well with men who prefer to believe that love and attraction exist in perfect harmony. Love and attraction can exist in harmony, but to have love you must first have attraction. It's a classic case of the chicken or the egg, which comes first? If your goal is to build attraction with women, it's crucial to separate the sweet, tender nature of love from the harsh reality of attraction. Love does exist, and it does grow out of attraction, but if you think you must be sweet, caring, and kind to win a woman's heart, you're sure to be disappointed.

Throughout this book, we've explored a multitude of ways to create, build, and maintain attraction. One area, however, we're yet to touch on is how to make yourself irresistible to women—to find the elusive X-factor in attraction. We know the X-factor exists, but for most men, any attempt to harness the power of attraction and channel its energy remains elusive. The X-factor continues to remain an abstract concept, in much the same way that nuclear fission remained an abstract concept until the day Trinity—the first atomic bomb—exploded into reality in 1945. Right now, you hold in your hands all the concepts and theories of attraction. Bringing these theories into reality, however, requires its own kind of nuclear fission. For this to happen, you must be able to turn theory into reality by smashing abstract concepts together like atoms. Only then, when you look into the blast crater can you catch a glimpse of the elusive X factor—attitude. Attitude is everything.

Men who are smart, handsome, educated, and who understand key concepts of attraction often come to me with the complaint that women still don't find them attractive. Women often tell these men how "nice" they are, effectively telling these men that they have no attraction for them whatsoever. Men who are considered anti-seductive, lack that all-important element of attraction—attitude. They smile too much; they're too nice; they're unsure of themselves; they communicate with weak words like "perhaps," "maybe," and "possibly," words that mirror the uncertainty of their mind. When women snap at them, act bitchy, and try to push them around, these men tolerate the abuse without putting up the slightest amount of resistance.

Bringing an edge to your character doesn't mean being an asshole, it means eradicating your desire to please and be nice. If a woman calls you a "nice guy," take it as an insult not a compliment. If a woman has the audacity to call you "nice" you mustn't respond with "thanks," instead, you must respond by telling her to "shut the fuck up."

"What?" She says, shocked by your crude response.

"Just kidding."

"Uhhh." She looks around, feeling slightly uncomfortable.

"Still think I'm nice?"

She laughs. Maybe not, but you're certainly a lot more attractive. As we dig deeper into the depths of attraction, it becomes clear that women adore men who score high on dark triad traits.[120] These dark triad traits include narcissism, Machiavellianism, and psychopathy. Men who score high on dark triad traits are usually more confident and selfish than their less self-assured peers. They're also more likely to be self-interested and attempt to manipulate and exploit other people without any sense of guilt or remorse. Among such men, there's a dark, apathetic quality that often underpins their relationships with women; a quality that challenges women and keeps them around despite the man's "asshole" behavior. Research has found evidence to suggest that men who possess dark triad traits are more likely to date more women, have more sex, and be seen as more attractive.[121]

A study published in the *Journal of Evolutionary Psychology* suggests that self-absorbed, narcissistic men are more desirable for both one-night stands and short-term relationships.[122] If research into attraction is anything to go by, women are more attracted to men who wear flashy, stylish clothes, have humorous verbal expressions, and display open, confident body language—all qualities that narcissists possess in abundance.[123] It's for this reason that narcissists strike such a powerful first impression: they are natural born charmers who stand out from the crowd.[124]

Another trait that makes dark triad men so appealing is their self-absorbed nature. The dark triad man puts himself and his needs first. Taken to an extreme, men who score high on dark triad traits are often highly destructive, not just to themselves but to the people around them. And even though it's estimated that approximately one percent of the world's population is psychopathic, the majority of psychopaths are fully functional, productive members of society. Instead of becoming serial killers and mass murderers, as depicted by Hollywood, most "functional psychopaths" live highly productive lives, only resorting to manipulation and deception to get what they want.

The benefits of selfishness and narcissism mustn't be underestimated. The man who's selfish and self-centered is much more likely to be successful in life. He's more likely to get promoted, get what he wants, and acquire more skills and knowledge along the way. He's more likely to start his own business. And he's more likely to acquire a greater number of assets and resources in the process. This is part of the reason why women find dark triad men so attractive.[125] Dark triad men are not only more resourceful and assertive—two important components of attraction—they're also more likely to be charming and humorous. Another aspect that makes dark triad men so alluring is their propensity to take risks and go after what they want without fear of reprisal. This was corroborated by a study published in the *Personality and Social Psychology Bulletin*. The study found that men who displayed nonconformist traits such as risk-taking and assertiveness were seen as more attractive.[126] After all, in a world where most people are conformist, the man who's unafraid to stand out is a unique and valuable commodity.

Women want men who have a sense of purpose and ambition. The last thing a woman wants is a man who's focused exclusively on her and her erratic emotions. A woman must feel safe pouring her emotions into you without having to worry that you'll fold under pressure. In the same way, you wouldn't want to keep your money in a bank that isn't safe and secure, women don't want to invest their emotions into men who are weak and vulnerable. This doesn't mean you should go out of your way to be mean or obnoxious. Research shows that women aren't attracted to aggressive men who commit reckless acts of violence, they're attracted to assertive men who have the courage to go after what they want in life. A man's innate aggression is only valued when it comes to protecting his loved ones from outside aggressors. Are evil, aggressive men attractive? The answer is *no*. Research has confirmed that men who were "known to be evil" or "mean," regardless of appearance, were classified as highly "unattractive" by both men and women.[127]

As you read this, you might start to feel unsettled, wondering if you really have to be an "asshole" or selfish to build attraction with women. In the world of seduction, being selfish and self-centered is not as bad as it sounds. It simply means focusing on *you* as opposed to focusing on *her*. What's more, displaying dark triad traits communicates to women that you have the ability to stand up for yourself and focus on what's important in life: you, your goals, and your mission. You must have purpose, you must have goals, and you must have a mission to give your life meaning. It doesn't matter whether you want to become a doctor, artist, businessman, entrepreneur, athlete, soldier, or entertainer. If you can harness the dark triad traits that already exist within you, you'll not only achieve greater focus and clarity, you're much more likely to be successful as well.

The man who fails with women is the man who seeks out relationships to give his life meaning. Without clear goals and a sense of purpose, you'll be left feeling unsatisfied, and no amount of love or tenderness from a woman will make you feel better. That's not to say that having a loving relationship with a woman is impossible, far from it. In fact, I'm here to tell you that you can have love, you can have sex, you can have trust, and you can have loyalty. But before you have any of these things, you must first build attraction. After all, the purpose of this book is not to show you how attraction *should be*, it's to show you how attraction *really is*. And once you appreciate and understand the true nature of attraction, you can have all the love, sex, and intimacy your heart desires.

REFERENCES

1. Tifferet, S., Kruger, D. J., Bar-Lev, O., & Zeller, S. (2013). Dog ownership increases attractiveness and attenuates perceptions of short-term mating strategy in cad-like men. *Journal of Evolutionary Psychology, 11*(3), 121-129. doi:10.1556/jep.11.2013.3.2

2. Guéguen, N. (2014). Men's music ability and attractiveness to women in a real-life courtship context. *Psychology of Music, 42*(4), 545-549. doi:10.1177/0305735613482025

3. Burriss, R. P., Rowland, H. M., & Little, A. C. (2009). Facial scarring enhances men's attractiveness for short-term relationships. *Personality and Individual Differences, 46*(2), 213-217. doi:10.1016/j.paid.2008.09.029

4. NVSS - National Marriage and Divorce Rate Trends. (n.d.). Retrieved from https://www.cdc.gov/nchs/nvss/marriage_divorce_tables.htm

5. Hamermesh, D. S. (2013). Beauty pays: Why attractive people are more successful. Princeton, NJ: Princeton University Press.

6. Schützwohl, A., Fuchs, A., McKibbin, W. F., & Shackelford, T. K. (2009). How Willing Are You to Accept Sexual Requests from Slightly Unattractive to Exceptionally Attractive Imagined Requestors? *Human Nature, 20*(3), 282-293. doi:10.1007/s12110009906733

7. Soler, C., Núñez, M., Gutiérrez, R., Núñez, J., Medina, P., Sancho, M., … Núñez, A. (2003). Facial attractiveness in men provides clues to semen quality.

Evolution and Human Behavior, 24(3), 199-207.
doi:10.1016/s1090-5138(03)00013-8

8. Felmlee, D. H. (1995). Fatal Attractions: Affection and Disaffection in Intimate Relationships. *Journal of Social and Personal Relationships, 12*(2), 295-311.
doi:10.1177/0265407595122009

9. Karandashev, V., & Fata, B. (2014). Change in Physical Attraction in Early Romantic Relationships. *Interpersona: An International Journal on Personal Relationships, 8*(2), 257-267.
doi:10.5964/ijpr.v8i2.167

10.   Shepperd, J. A., & Strathman, A. J. (1989). Attractiveness and Height. *Personality and Social Psychology Bulletin, 15*(4), 617-627. doi:10.1177/0146167289154014

11.   Vandello, J. A., Ransom, S., Hettinger, V. E., & Askew, K. (2009). Men's misperceptions about the acceptability and attractiveness of aggression. *Journal of Experimental Social Psychology, 45*(6), 1209-1219.
doi:10.1016/j.jesp.2009.08.006

12.   Vincke, E. (2016). The Young Male Cigarette and Alcohol Syndrome. *Evolutionary Psychology, 14*(1), 147470491663161. doi:10.1177/1474704916631615

13.   Frederick, D. A., & Haselton, M. G. (2007). Why Is Muscularity Sexy? Tests of the Fitness Indicator Hypothesis. *Personality and Social Psychology Bulletin, 33*(8), 1167-1183. doi:10.1177/0146167207303022

14.   Frederick, D., & Haselton, M. (n.d.). Do evolved perceptual biases influence women's preferences of different male body types? *PsycEXTRA Dataset.*
doi:10.1037/e633912013-813

15.   Silver foxes: Why going gray is sexy. (n.d.). Retrieved from http://www.match.com/magazine/article/1458/

silver-foxes-why-gray-is-sexy

16.   Rivas, A. (n.d.). Going Bald Named The Greatest
Aging Fear By 94% Of Men. Retrieved from
http://www.medicaldaily.com/going-bald-named-
greatest-aging-fear-94-men-257516

17.   Mannes, A. (n.d.). Shorn Scalps and Perceptions of
Male Dominance. *PsycEXTRA Dataset.*
doi:10.1037/e570052013-044

18.   Dixson, B. J., & Brooks, R. C. (2013). The role of
facial hair in women's perceptions of men's attractiveness,
health, masculinity and parenting abilities. *Evolution and
Human Behavior, 34*(3), 236-241.
doi:10.1016/j.evolhumbehav.2013.02.003

19.   Dixson, B. J., & Rantala, M. J. (2015). The Role of
Facial and Body Hair Distribution in Women's Judgments
of Men's Sexual Attractiveness. *Archives of Sexual Behavior,
45*(4), 877-889. doi:10.1007/s10508-015-0588-z

20.   Veale, D., Miles, S., Bramley, S., Muir, G., &
Hodsoll, J. (2015). Am I normal? A systematic review and
construction of nomograms for flaccid and erect penis
length and circumference in up to 15,521 men. *BJU
International, 115*(6), 978-986. doi:10.1111/bju.13010

21.   Dixson, B. J., Dixson, A. F., Bishop, P. J., &
Parish, A. (2009). Human Physique and Sexual
Attractiveness in Men and Women: A New Zealand–U.S.
Comparative Study. *Archives of Sexual Behavior, 39*(3), 798-
806. doi:10.1007/s10508-008-9441-y

22.   Male Attractiveness Over Time. (n.d.). Retrieved
from http://socionist.blogspot.com/2011/11/male-
attractiveness-over-time.html

23.   Moore, F., Cassidy, C., & Perrett, D. I. (2010). The Effects of Control of Resources on Magnitudes of Sex Differences in Human Mate Preferences. *Evolutionary Psychology, 8*(4), 147470491000800. doi:10.1177/147470491000800412

24.   Moore, F., Cassidy, C., & Perrett, D. I. (2010). The Effects of Control of Resources on Magnitudes of Sex Differences in Human Mate Preferences. *Evolutionary Psychology, 8*(4), 147470491000800. doi:10.1177/147470491000800412

25.   Zuckerman, M., & Driver, R. E. (1988). What sounds beautiful is good: The vocal attractiveness stereotype. *Journal of Nonverbal Behavior, 13*(2), 67-82. doi:10.1007/bf00990791

26.   Wallrabenstein, I., Gerber, J., Rasche, S., Croy, I., Kurtenbach, S., Hummel, T., & Hatt, H. (2015). The smelling of Hedione results in sex-differentiated human brain activity. *NeuroImage, 113*, 365-373. doi:10.1016/j.neuroimage.2015.03.029

27.   Mak, G. K., Enwere, E. K., Gregg, C., Pakarainen, T., Poutanen, M., Huhtaniemi, I., & Weiss, S. (2007). Male pheromone-stimulated neurogenesis in the adult female brain: possible role in mating behavior. *Nature Neuroscience, 10*(8), 1003-1011. doi:10.1038/nn1928

28.   Saxton, T., Lyndon, A., Little, A., & Roberts, S. (2008). Evidence that androstadienone, a putative human chemosignal, modulates women's attributions of men's attractiveness. *Hormones and Behavior, 54*(5), 597-601. doi:10.1016/j.yhbeh.2008.06.001

29.   Fialová, J., Roberts, S. C., & Havlíček, J. (2016). Consumption of garlic positively affects hedonic perception of axillary body odor. *Appetite, 97*, 8-15.

doi:10.1016/j.appet.2015.11.001

30.   Craig Roberts, S., Little, A. C., Lyndon, A.,
Roberts, J., Havlicek, J., & Wright, R. L. (2009).
Manipulation of body odor alters men's self-confidence
and judgments of their visual attractiveness by women.
International Journal of Cosmetic Science, 31(1), 47-54.
doi:10.1111/j.1468-2494.2008.00477.x

31.   Buller, D. J. (2006). Adapting minds: Evolutionary
psychology and the persistent quest for human nature.
Cambridge, MA: MIT.

32.   Well Dressed Men Survey. (n.d.). Retrieved from
https://www.keltonglobal.com/in-the-media/should-you-
still-dress-to-impress-at-work/

33.   Elliot, A. J., Niesta Kayser, D., Greitemeyer, T.,
Lichtenfeld, S., Gramzow, R. H., Maier, M. A., & Liu, H.
(2010). Red, rank, and romance in women viewing men.
Journal of Experimental Psychology: General, 139(3), 399-417.
doi:10.1037/a0019689

34.   Roberts, S. C., Owen, R. C., & Havlicek, J. (2010).
Distinguishing between Perceiver and Wearer Effects in
Clothing Color-Associated Attributions. *Evolutionary
Psychology, 8*(3), 147470491000800.
doi:10.1177/147470491000800304

35.   Elder, G. H. (1969). Appearance and Education in
Marriage Mobility. *American Sociological Review, 34*(4), 519.
doi:10.2307/2091961

36.   Kniffin, K. M., & Wilson, D. S. (2004). The effect of
nonphysical traits on the perception of physical
attractiveness. *Evolution and Human Behavior, 25*(2), 88-101.
doi:10.1016/s1090-5138(04)00006-6

37.   Bryan, A. D., Webster, G. D., & Mahaffey, A. L. (2011). The Big, the Rich, and the Powerful: Physical, Financial, and Social Dimensions of Dominance in Mating and Attraction. *Personality and Social Psychology Bulletin, 37*(3), 365-382. doi:10.1177/0146167210395604

38.   Barber, N. (1995). The evolutionary psychology of physical attractiveness: Sexual selection and human morphology. *Ethology and Sociobiology, 16*(5), 395-424. doi:10.1016/0162-3095(95)00068-2

39.   Sadalla, E. K., Kenrick, D. T., & Vershure, B. (1987). Dominance and heterosexual attraction. *Journal of Personality and Social Psychology, 52*(4), 730-738. doi:10.1037//0022-3514.52.4.730

40.   Snyder, J. K., Kirkpatrick, L. A., & Barrett, H. C. (2008). The dominance dilemma: Do women really prefer dominant mates? *Personal Relationships, 15*(4), 425-444. doi:10.1111/j.1475-6811.2008.00208.x

41.   Wu, K., Chen, C., Moyzis, R. K., Greenberger, E., & Yu, Z. (2016). Gender Interacts with Opioid Receptor Polymorphism A118G and Serotonin Receptor Polymorphism −1438 A/G on Speed-Dating Success. *Human Nature, 27*(3), 244-260. doi:10.1007/s12110-016-9257-8

42.   Van Kleef, G. A., Homan, A. C., Finkenauer, C., Gündemir, S., & Stamkou, E. (2011). Breaking the Rules to Rise to Power. *Social Psychological and Personality Science, 2*(5), 500-507. doi:10.1177/1948550611398416

43.   White, G. L., & Kight, T. D. (1984). Misattribution of arousal and attraction: Effects of salience of explanations for arousal. *Journal of Experimental Social Psychology, 20*, 55-64. doi:10.1016/0022-1031(84)90012-X

44.   Dutton, D. G., & Aron, A. P. (1974). Some evidence for heightened sexual attraction under conditions of high anxiety. *Journal of Personality and Social Psychology, 30,* 510-517. doi:10.1037/h0037031

45.   Kleinke, C., Meeker, F., & Staneski, R. (1986). Preference for opening lines: Comparing ratings by men and women. *Sex Roles, 15,* 585-600. doi:10.1007/bf00288216

46.   Bale, C., Morrison, R., & Caryl, P. (2006). Chat-up lines as male sexual displays. *Personality and Individual Differences, 40,* 655-664. doi:10.1016/j.paid.2005.07.016

47.   Clark, R. (1989). Gender Differences in Receptivity to Sexual Offers. *Journal of Psychology & Human Sexuality, 2*(1), 39-55. doi:10.1300/j056v02n01_04

48.   Guéguen, N. (2011). Effects of Solicitor Sex and Attractiveness on Receptivity to Sexual Offers: A Field Study. *Archives of Sexual Behavior, 40*(5), 915-919. doi:10.1007/s10508-011-9750-4

49.   Pease, A. (2014). Body language: How to read others' thoughts by their gestures. Sheldon Press.

50.   Pease, A. A. (2017). The Definitive Book of Body Language. Bantam.

51.   Perilloux, C., Easton, J. A., & Buss, D. M. (2012). The Misperception of Sexual Interest. *Psychological Science, 23*(2), 146-151. doi:10.1177/0956797611424162

52.   Vacharkulksemsuk, T., Reit, E., Khambatta, P., Eastwick, P. W., Finkel, E. J., & Carney, D. R. (2016). Dominant, open nonverbal displays are attractive at zero-acquaintance. *Proceedings of the National Academy of Sciences, 113*(15), 4009-4014. doi:10.1073/pnas.1508932113

53.   Murphy, N. A. (2007). Appearing Smart: The Impression Management of Intelligence, Person Perception Accuracy, and Behavior in Social Interaction. *Personality and Social Psychology Bulletin, 33*(3), 325-339. doi:10.1177/0146167206294871

54.   Fink, B., Weege, B., Neave, N., Pham, M. N., & Shackelford, T. K. (2015). Integrating body movement into attractiveness research. *Frontiers in Psychology, 6.* doi:10.3389/fpsyg.2015.00220

55.   Thoresen, J. C., Vuong, Q. C., & Atkinson, A. P. (2012). First impressions: Gait cues drive reliable trait judgments. *Cognition, 124*(3), 261-271. doi:10.1016/j.cognition.2012.05.018

56.   Bray, C. (2012). Sean Connery: A biography. New York: Pegasus Books.

57.   Doob, A. N., & Gross, A. E. (1968). Status of Frustrator as an Inhibitor of Horn-Honking Responses. *The Journal of Social Psychology, 76*(2), 213-218. doi:10.1080/00224545.1968.9933615

58.   Tracy, J. L., & Beall, A. T. (2011). Happy guys finish last: The impact of emotion expressions on sexual attraction. *Emotion, 11*(6), 1379-1387. doi:10.1037/a0022902

59.   Tracy, J. L., & Beall, A. T. (2011). Happy guys finish last: The impact of emotion expressions on sexual attraction. *Emotion, 11*(6), 1379-1387. doi:10.1037/a0022902

60.   Naumann, L. P., Vazire, S., Rentfrow, P. J., & Gosling, S. D. (2009). Personality Judgments Based on Physical Appearance. *Personality and Social Psychology Bulletin, 35*(12), 1661-1671. doi:10.1177/0146167209346309

61.   Petraitis, J. M., Lampman, C. B., Boeckmann, R. J., & Falconer, E. M. (2014). Sex differences in the attractiveness of hunter-gatherer and modern risks. *Journal of Applied Social Psychology, 44*(6), 442-453. doi:10.1111/jasp.12237

62.   Muise, A., Christofides, E., & Desmarais, S. (2009). More Information than You Ever Wanted: Does Facebook Bring Out the Green-Eyed Monster of Jealousy? *CyberPsychology & Behavior, 12*(4), 441-444. doi:10.1089/cpb.2008.0263

63.   Rodeheffer, C. D., Proffitt Leyva, R. P., & Hill, S. E. (2016). Attractive Female Romantic Partners Provide a Proxy for Unobservable Male Qualities. *Evolutionary Psychology, 14*(2), 147470491665214. doi:10.1177/1474704916652144

64.   Dunn, M. J., & Searle, R. (2010). Effect of manipulated prestige-car ownership on both sex attractiveness ratings. *British Journal of Psychology, 101*(1), 69-80. doi:10.1348/000712609x417319

65.   Dunn, M. J., & Hill, A. (2014). Manipulated luxury-apartment ownership enhances opposite-sex attraction in females but not males. *Journal of Evolutionary Psychology, 12*(1), 1-17. doi:10.1556/jep.12.2014.1.1

66.   Walker, D., & Vul, E. (2014). Hierarchical Encoding Makes Individuals in a Group Seem More Attractive. *Psychological Science, 25*(1), 230-235. doi:10.1177/0956797613497969

67.   Jones, B. C., DeBruine, L. M., Little, A. C., Burriss, R. P., & Feinberg, D. R. (2007). Social transmission of face preferences among humans. *Proceedings of the Royal Society B: Biological Sciences, 274*(1611), 899-903. doi:10.1098/rspb.2006.0205

68. Vakirtzis, A., & Roberts, S. C. (2012). Do women really like taken men? Results from a large questionnaire study. *Journal of Social, Evolutionary, and Cultural Psychology*, *6*(1), 50-65. doi:10.1037/h0099225

69. Waynforth, D. (2007). Mate Choice Copying in Humans. *Human Nature, 18*(3), 264-271. doi:10.1007/s12110-007-9004-2

70. Whitchurch, E. R., Wilson, T. D., & Gilbert, D. T. (2011). "He Loves Me, He Loves Me Not…" *Psychological Science, 22*(2), 172-175. doi:10.1177/0956797610393745

71. Aronson, E., & Linder, D. (1965). Gain and loss of esteem as determinants of interpersonal attractiveness. *Journal of Experimental Social Psychology, 1*(2), 156-171

72. Birnbaum, G. E., Ein-Dor, T., Reis, H. T., & Segal, N. (2014). Why Do Men Prefer Nice Women? Gender Typicality Mediates the Effect of Responsiveness on Perceived Attractiveness in Initial Acquaintanceships. *Personality and Social Psychology Bulletin, 40*(10), 1341-1353. doi:10.1177/0146167214543879

73. Birnbaum, G. E., Ein-Dor, T., Reis, H. T., & Segal, N. (2014). Why Do Men Prefer Nice Women? Gender Typicality Mediates the Effect of Responsiveness on Perceived Attractiveness in Initial Acquaintanceships. *Personality and Social Psychology Bulletin, 40*(10), 1341-1353. doi:10.1177/0146167214543879

74. Whitchurch, E. R., Wilson, T. D., & Gilbert, D. T. (2011). "He Loves Me, He Loves Me Not…" *Psychological Science, 22*(2), 172-175. doi:10.1177/0956797610393745

75. Okimoto, T. G., Wenzel, M., & Hedrick, K. (2012). Refusing to apologize can have psychological benefits (and we issue no mea culpa for this research finding). *European Journal of Social Psychology, 43*(1), 22-31.

doi:10.1002/ejsp.1901

76.   Quoidbach, J., Hansenne, M., & Mottet, C. (2008). Personality and mental time travel: A differential approach to autonoetic consciousness. *Consciousness and Cognition, 17*(4), 1082-1092. doi:10.1016/j.concog.2008.04.002

77.   Donahue, J. K., & Green, M. C. (2016). A good story: Men's storytelling ability affects their attractiveness and perceived status. *Personal Relationships, 23*(2), 199-213. doi:10.1111/pere.12120

78.   Dominance, prosocial orientation, and female preferences: Do nice guys really finish last? (1995). *Journal of Personality and Social Psychology, 68*(3), 427-440. doi:10.1037//0022-3514.68.3.427

79.   Dominance, prosocial orientation, and female preferences: Do nice guys really finish last? (1995). *Journal of Personality and Social Psychology, 68*(3), 427-440. doi:10.1037//0022-3514.68.3.427

80.   Donahue, J. K., & Green, M. C. (2016). A good story: Men's storytelling ability affects their attractiveness and perceived status. *Personal Relationships, 23*(2), 199-213. doi:10.1111/pere.12120

81.   Collins, N. L., & Miller, L. C. (1994). Self-disclosure and liking: A meta-analytic review. *Psychological Bulletin, 116*(3), 457-475. doi:10.1037//0033-2909.116.3.457

82.   Aronson, E., & Worchel, P. (1966). Similarity versus liking as determinants of interpersonal attractiveness. *Psychonomic Science, 5*(4), 157-158. doi:10.3758/bf03328329

83.   Guéguen, N. (2007). Courtship compliance: The effect of touch on women's behavior. *Social Influence, 2*(2), 81-97. doi:10.1080/15534510701316177

84. Burgoon, J. K., Walther, J. B., & Baesler, E. J. (1992). Interpretations, Evaluations, and Consequences of Interpersonal Touch. *Human Communication Research, 19*(2), 237-263. doi:10.1111/j.1468-2958.1992.tb00301.x

85. Effect of mutual gaze and touch on attraction, mood, and cardiovascular reactivity. *Journal of Research in Personality, 27,* 170-183.)

86. Jonason, P. K., Garcia, J. R., Webster, G. D., Li, N. P., & Fisher, H. E. (2015). Relationship Dealbreakers. *Personality and Social Psychology Bulletin, 41*(12), 1697-1711. doi:10.1177/0146167215609064

87. Jonason, P. K., & Li, N. P. (in press). Playing hard-to-get: Manipulating one's perceived availability as a mate. *European Journal of Personality.*

88. Georgiadis, J. R., Simone Reinders, A., Van der Graaf, F. H., Paans, A. M., & Kortekaas, R. (2007). Brain activation during human male ejaculation revisited. *NeuroReport, 18*(6), 553-557. doi:10.1097/wnr.0b013e3280b10bfe

89. Blumstein, P., & Schwartz, P. (1985). *American couples: Money, work, sex.* New York: Pocket Books.

90. Puts, D. A., Welling, L. L., Burriss, R. P., & Dawood, K. (2012). Men's masculinity and attractiveness predict their female partners' reported orgasm frequency and timing. *Evolution and Human Behavior, 33*(1), 1-9. doi:10.1016/j.evolhumbehav.2011.03.003

91. Jonason, P. K., & Li, N. P. (in press). Playing hard-to-get: Manipulating one's perceived availability as a mate. *European Journal of Personality.*

92. Cialdini, R. B. (1985). Influence: How and why people agree to things. New York: Quill.

93.   Wu, K., Chen, C., Moyzis, R. K., Greenberger, E., & Yu, Z. (2016). Gender Interacts with Opioid Receptor Polymorphism A118G and Serotonin Receptor Polymorphism −1438 A/G on Speed-Dating Success. *Human Nature, 27*(3), 244-260. doi:10.1007/s12110-016-9257-8

94.   Chick, G., Yarnal, C., & Purrington, A. (2012). Play and Mate Preference - Testing the Signal Theory of Adult Playfulness. *American Journal of Play, 4*(4), 407-440.

95.   Janz, P., Pepping, C. A., & Halford, W. K. (2015). Individual differences in dispositional mindfulness and initial romantic attraction: A speed dating experiment. *Personality and Individual Differences, 82,* 14-19. doi:10.1016/j.paid.2015.02.025

96.   Tornquist, M., & Chiappe, D. (2015). Effects of Humor Production, Humor Receptivity, and Physical Attractiveness on Partner Desirability. *Evolutionary Psychology, 13*(4), 147470491560874. doi:10.1177/1474704915608744

97.   Vrticka, P., Neely, M., Walter Shelly, E., Black, J. M., & Reiss, A. L. (2013). Sex differences during humor appreciation in child-sibling pairs. *Social Neuroscience, 8*(4), 291-304. doi:10.1080/17470919.2013.794751

98.   Guéguen, N. (2010). Men's Sense of Humor and Women's Responses to Courtship Solicitations: An Experimental Field Study 1. *Psychological Reports, 107*(1), 145-156. doi:10.2466/pr0.107.1.145-156

99.   Birnbaum, G. E., Ein-Dor, T., Reis, H. T., & Segal, N. (2014). Why Do Men Prefer Nice Women? Gender Typicality Mediates the Effect of Responsiveness on Perceived Attractiveness in Initial Acquaintanceships. *Personality and Social Psychology Bulletin, 40*(10), 1341-1353.

doi:10.1177/0146167214543879

100. Shen, L., Fishbach, A., & Hsee, C. K. (2015). The Motivating-Uncertainty Effect: Uncertainty Increases Resource Investment in the Process of Reward Pursuit. *Journal of Consumer Research, 41*(5), 1301-1315. doi:10.1086/679418

101. Whitchurch, E. R., Wilson, T. D., & Gilbert, D. T. (2011). "He Loves Me, He Loves Me Not…" *Psychological Science, 22*(2), 172-175. doi:10.1177/0956797610393745

102. Leary, M. R., Rogers, P. A., Canfield, R. W., & Coe, C. (1986). Boredom in interpersonal encounters: Antecedents and social implications. *Journal of Personality and Social Psychology, 51*(5), 968-975. doi:10.1037//0022-3514.51.5.968

103. Bellis, M. A. (2005). Measuring paternal discrepancy and its public health consequences. *Journal of Epidemiology & Community Health, 59*(9), 749-754. doi:10.1136/jech.2005.036517

104. McClintock, E. A. (2014). Beauty and Status. *American Sociological Review, 79*(4), 575-604. doi:10.1177/0003122414536391

105. Perel, E. (2006). Mating in captivity: Reconciling the erotic + the domestic. New York: HarperCollins.

106. Harrison, M. A., & Shortall, J. C. (2011). Women and Men in Love: Who Really Feels It and Says It First? *The Journal of Social Psychology, 151*(6), 727-736. doi:10.1080/00224545.2010.522626

107. Seligman, M. E. (1971). Phobias and preparedness. *Behavior Therapy, 2*(3), 307-320. doi:10.1016/s0005-7894(71)80064-3

108. Worchel, S., Lee, J., & Adewole, A. (1975). Effects of supply and demand on ratings of object value. *Journal of Personality and Social Psychology, 32*(5), 906-914. doi:10.1037//0022-3514.32.5.906

109. Schmidt, U., & Zank, H. (2005). What is Loss Aversion? *Journal of Risk and Uncertainty, 30*(2), 157-167. doi:10.1007/s11166-005-6564-6

110. Jonason, P. K., & Li, N. P. (in press). Playing hard-to-get: Manipulating one's perceived availability as a mate. *European Journal of Personality.*

111. Bleske-Rechek, A., Somers, E., Micke, C., Erickson, L., Matteson, L., Stocco, C., … Ritchie, L. (2012). Benefit or burden? Attraction in cross-sex friendship. *Journal of Social and Personal Relationships, 29*(5), 569-596. doi:10.1177/0265407512443611

112. Kreager, D. A., Molloy, L. E., Moody, J., & Feinberg, M. E. (2015). Friends First? The Peer Network Origins of Adolescent Dating. *Journal of Research on Adolescence, 26*(2), 257-269. doi:10.1111/jora.12189

113. Belk, R. W., & Coon, G. S. (1991). Can't buy me love: Dating, money, and gifts. *Advances in Consumer Research, 18*, 521-527.

114. Horan, S. M., & Booth-Butterfield, M. (2010). Investing in affection: An investigation of affection exchange theory and relational qualities. *Communication Quarterly, 58*(4), 394-413.

115. Conley, T. D., & Rabinowitz, J. L. (2009). The Devaluation of Relationships (not Individuals): The Case of Dyadic Relationship Stigmatization. *Journal of Applied Social Psychology, 39*(4), 918-944. doi:10.1111/j.1559-1816.2009.00466.x

116. Meston, C., & Frohlich, P. (2003). The self-esteem roller coaster: Adult attachment moderates the impact of daily feedback. *Archives of Sexual Behavior, 32*(6), 537-544.

117. McKinney, K. (n.d.). The Effects of Adrenaline on Arousal and Attraction. Retrieved from http://www.mckendree.edu/academics/scholars/issue17/mckinney.htm

118. Dutton, D. G., & Aron, A. P. (1974). Some evidence for heightened sexual attraction under conditions of high anxiety. *Journal of Personality and Social Psychology, 30*(4), 510-517. doi:10.1037/h0037031

119. Hedges, C. (2003). War is a force that gives us meaning. New York: A.A. Knopf.

120. Carter, G. L., Campbell, A. C., & Muncer, S. (2014). The Dark Triad personality: Attractiveness to women. *Personality and Individual Differences, 56,* 57-61. doi:10.1016/j.paid.2013.08.021

121. Hare, R. D., Babiak, P., McLaren, T. P., & Tantor Media. (2011). Snakes in suits: When psychopaths go to work. Old Saybrook, Ct.: Tantor Media.

122. Moore, D., Wigby, S., English, S., Wong, S., Székely, T., & Harrison, F. (2013). Selflessness is sexy: reported helping behavior increases desirability of men and women as long-term sexual partners. *BMC Evolutionary Biology, 13*(1), 182. doi:10.1186/1471-2148-13-182

123. Farrelly, D., Clemson, P., & Guthrie, M. (2016). Are Women's Mate Preferences for Altruism Also Influenced by Physical Attractiveness? *Evolutionary Psychology, 14*(1), 147470491562369. doi:10.1177/1474704915623698

124. Back, M.D., Schmukle, S.C., & Egloff, B. (1010). Why are narcissists so charming at first sight? Decoding the

narcissism-popularity link at zero acquaintance. *Journal of Personality and Social Psychology, 98,* 132-145.

125. Moore, D., Wigby, S., English, S., Wong, S., Székely, T., & Harrison, F. (2013). Selflessness is sexy: reported helping behavior increases desirability of men and women as long-term sexual partners. *BMC Evolutionary Biology, 13*(1), 182. doi:10.1186/1471-2148-13-182

126. Hornsey, M. J., Wellauer, R., McIntyre, J. C., & Barlow, F. K. (2015). A Critical Test of the Assumption That Men Prefer Conformist Women and Women Prefer Nonconformist Men. *Personality and Social Psychology Bulletin, 41*(6), 755-768. doi:10.1177/0146167215577366

127. Zhang, Y., Kong, F., Zhong, Y., & Kou, H. (2014). Personality manipulations: Do they modulate facial attractiveness ratings? *Personality and Individual Differences, 70,* 80-84. doi:10.1016/j.paid.2014.06.033